A GRANDAD'S LIFE

A GRANDAD'S LIFE

James K Humble OBE

A GRANDAD'S LIFE
James K Humble OBE
Copyright © 2008

First published 2008 by Cockasnook Books,
22 Whernside Road, Nottingham NG5 4LD
www.cockasnook.co.uk

Printed by The Russell Press,
Russell House, Bulwell Lane, Nottingham NG6 0BT
www.russellpress.com

ISBN 978-0-9557460-2-4

Cover illustration by eldest grandchild, James Paterson
(aged 9 at the time)

James Kenneth Humble aged one year, 1937.

This book is dedicated to my grandchildren: James, Ben, Alice, Sam, Thomas, Emily and Elliot. It is my perception of my family, my life and my memories. I recognise that people see things differently and apologise to those whose recollections may be different.

James Humble, 1st January 2008

CONTENTS

Introduction.. 9
First Impressions.. 10
Jim Humble... 13
My Family.. 15
My Grandparents....................................... 20
Great-Grandparents.................................. 25
Aunts and Uncles....................................... 30
Cousins.. 33
Early Friends.. 36
Early Memories... 38
Junior School... 46
Grammar School... 51
Working Holidays....................................... 55
Youthful Miscellany................................... 58
St John's Church... 62
Colts Rugby.. 64
Work and Career.. 65
National Service.. 67
Back in Oldham.. 72
Girlfriends.. 75
Rugby... 77
Courtship.. 81
Wedding.. 84
Nigeria... 86
Holidays.. 92
Daughters... 94
Croydon... 98
Office of Fair Trading............................... 101
Hague 9... 105
Metrication Board..................................... 107
National Metrological Coordinating Unit............... 110
LACOTS.. 111
Retirement... 115
Finally Freda.. 118
Photographs.. 121
Appendix A: Memories of My Mother.................... 131
Appendix B: Letters from Nigeria............................141
Very Last Word... 149
Family trees... 151

A GRANDAD'S LIFE

INTRODUCTION

On 8 May 2004 (my 68th birthday) my middle daughter Rebecca gave me a 'Grandparent's Book' to record memories of my life. I first updated it on the occasion of my 70th birthday at 'The Crown' in Norfolk. The original intention was to identify relatives and early memories but it has drifted towards being a résumé of key events in my life. Not quite what I intended.

My 70th was a perfect birthday memory, surrounded by the people I love most: my wife Freda (Nanny), my three daughters, six grandchildren and three sons-in-law. It was even better than my ninth birthday, 8 May 1945, when bunting and flags adorned my house and covered the country. I thought they were just for me but they were to celebrate the ending of the Second World War. They also meant my Royal Navy dad could come home from Australia where he had been stationed against a possible Japanese invasion. It was the beginning of a happy and enjoyable life.

Being 70 is amazing. My grandparents seemed like ancient dinosaurs. But now I empathise with the logo on one of my presents, a T-shirt which reads

"I'm not 70. I'm 18 with 52 years' experience."

Inside I still feel much as I felt in my youth. I am sure my grandchildren will feel the same.
It is truly amazing.

FIRST IMPRESSIONS

Three people were dominant in the first twenty plus years of my life: mother, father and maternal grandmother Tamar. Remarkable name, Tamar. She used to say it was the name of a harlot in the Bible. She was larger than life, a fearsome, sharp-tongued woman, fiercely protective and aggressively supportive of her family. She was consistently and totally hostile to neighbours, friends, other wings of the family, indeed the whole of the world. I think I might have got my supportive gene from her, but hope I have managed to avoid her unrelenting antagonism to the rest of society. I am sure that is right. I have rarely felt hostile to anyone and always presume people to have good intentions and motives.

I loved my dad, but he was very strict. Only ever gave one chance to obey. One word of reprimand and that was it. Grandchildren please note. But I recognised from an early age he was even-tempered, consistent and scrupulously fair. He also convinced me that 'if a job's worth doing, it's worth doing well' – an adage he repeated time and again whenever I flagged. I'm bound to say that I always think of him and his sayings when facing a difficult or unpleasant task. Many times it caused me to push on. Good old Dad.

My mother Alice gave me unswerving, unflinching and uncritical loving support. She seemed to be proud of whatever I did, the little things and the bigger ones. I hope I have passed that loving gene to my daughters... and that they, in turn, will continue to love and encourage their children. I am sure they will.

Looking back, a rather odd thing influenced the pattern of my life, influenced it disproportionately. It's a name. A name used by aunts, uncles and cousins when I was only nine or ten years old. A name which cropped up at school and later in the Navy. A name used at work, in my later career and which continues with some of our geriatric friends, bridge players and golfers. A name never used by my immediate family. It is 'Lucky Jim' or, to quote my favourite cousin, 'Jammy Jimmy'.

It was said so authoritatively and so frequently that at some early age I came to believe it was true. I believed I was especially charmed. And I did seem to win prizes, get promotions, miss disasters and do well compared with my peers. I was lucky with accidents and when bombs dropped nearby. I just enjoyed collecting the red-hot bits of shrapnel. When I reflect I can see that it affected my frame of mind on countless numbers of occasions. I always expect optimistic and favourable outcomes, including recently in 2003 and 2004 when there were setbacks that affected both Nanny and me: Alzheimer's and cancer.

If things don't look good I am relaxed, unworried… confident I will be the beneficiary of compensatory good fortune. Good luck. The expectations of the term 'Lucky Jim' led me to become an optimist. However, after seventy years I know that 'it's a good way to live a life'. I am just amazed that such a peripheral thing could be so significant.

But the single 'luckiest' bit of my life was to meet and marry Freda Holden, Nanny. And then to produce three lovely daughters – Josephine, Rebecca and Sarah – and for them to marry three fine, good men. My father-in-law, GF Holden, Mayor of Oldham, would have described each as upright, decent and honest. I agree. These unions have now produced the seven most handsome, beautiful, intelligent, clever, well-behaved, quiet, non-wriggly, co-operative and 'lucky' children any grandad could ever wish for.

They are all brilliant. I love them all. On my 70th birthday one daughter asked me what present I really wanted. Well, apart from just wanting all my immediate family to be together on the family photo… An inspired idea: what I really really want is for my children and grandchildren to carry on being close, loving and supportive to each other. I want them to seize opportunities to recreate days like my birthday, occasions when cousins meet and enjoy each other's company. Otherwise it's so easy to let time and circumstance force families apart. Everyone's life then becomes much the poorer.

Let me finish this beginning by misquoting President JF Kennedy when he gave hope, excitement and vision in 1960 to the whole of my generation: "Think not what your *family* can do for you. Think only what you can do to *love and support* your *family.*"

JIM HUMBLE

I begin with ME. My full name is James Kenneth Humble. I was born on 8 May 1936 in the Greenacres Nursing Home, Oldham, Lancashire. Oldham was the greatest cotton spinning town in the world with 320 mills each belching black smoke into the atmosphere. There were also 365 pubs – one for each day of the year. I visited every one. The other big news in 1936 was the abdication of the King.

Throughout my early life I was known as Jimmy and later Jim. I became a part-time professional Rugby League player in 1959 but spent my main career in trading standards, starting as a weights and measures inspector in Oldham in 1952. I married Freda Holden in 1962 and then continued my career for nearly four years with the Nigerian Government in Lagos and Kano.

We returned to the UK in 1966 and I was initially Deputy Chief Trading Standards Officer in Croydon, becoming Chief Officer in 1971. In 1973 I was appointed Deputy Director of Consumer Affairs in a new powerful government agency, the Office of Fair Trading. In 1979 I became Director of the Metrication Board, which was abolished when Margaret Thatcher became Prime Minister. However, I moved seamlessly to become Director of the National Metrological Coordinating Body and in 1982 also acquired chief executiveship of LACOTS (Local Authority Coordinating Body on Food and Trading Standards). I loved every bit of every job and eventually retired in 1998 with forty-six years of pensionable service.

However, the great delights of my life have been my three daughters: Josephine Clare (1964), Rebecca Jane (1965) and Sarah Louise (1966), who have now produced the seven lovely grandchildren, James, Ben and Sam Paterson, Alice and Thomas Munson, Emily Cordle and, in June 2007, Elliot Cordle, to whom I have dedicated these memories.

MY FAMILY

My mother Alice, nee Rhodes (22 Oct 1909 – 26 Nov 1992), was born in Oldham. She worked as a tailoress after she left school at fourteen years of age and was very artistic. Quite brilliant drawings. She was a clever girl but her mother Tamar refused to allow her to take the usual scholarship. Tamar said, "One's enough in any family." This referred to Alice's older brother Fred who became Secretary and Director of Dronsfield Brothers, Oldham. His company was the world leader in the manufacture of specialist cotton machinery. I learned from Fred's wife Ann, in 2000, that my mother was born with a very bad cleft palate and harelip. Her doctor 'sewed it up' when she was a few weeks old and was deemed to have done a magnificent job. Certainly I never noticed and it did not detract from her good looks in any way. Study her photos and you can tell.

My mother married my father Joseph on 12 August 1935. I was always referred to as a 'honeymoon baby', born nine months later. We lived at 208 Wellington Road, Oldham which they bought for £70 with a large mortgage. When I was thirteen we moved to a three-bedroomed house at 35 Oriel Avenue, Coppice, Oldham and later to 'the shop' at 54 Gainsborough Avenue.

My mother was unfailingly loving and supportive towards her children - all her family. She lacked confidence when Dad was around as he made every decision – quite normal in those days. In 1975 Dad was hospitalised after having the first of his three heart attacks. It was Easter 1975. Freda drove to Mevagissey with the girls and I got the train to Codsall,

Wolverhampton to where my parents had moved to be near Margaret, my sister. I was amazed by how much more confident and organised my mother had become within two or three traumatic days. That weekend she signed her first ever cheque. She was sixty-six years old and was clear and decisive about the future. Her confidence increased and the following year she wrote an unsentimental account of her early life for her godchild, my second daughter Rebecca. It is a clear description of a working-class family between the First and Second World Wars. I reproduce her account, in full, in Appendix A.

My mother died from leukaemia at the age of 83 years. She had been ill for only two days.

My father, Joseph Humble (19 Mar 1910 – 12 May 1993), was known by everyone as 'Joe' or 'Our Joe'. He was a butcher by trade and became Assistant Manager of the Oldham Industrial Coop Society before buying a retail grocery shop in Gainsborough Avenue, Oldham. His older siblings were Jenny, Fred and Jack, with a younger sister Dolly. He was awesomely hard-working, packed with energy and universally respected and liked. He was also a strict disciplinarian and ruled his family with a rod of iron. He was iron-willed and stoic about pain. In 1949 he had a bad knee injury from playing football and was told by the doctor he would need an operation to have the joint permanently stiffened. No way. He kept the joint moving by standing on a chair and dropping the full weight of his other leg to the floor. He bit into a leather purse and beads of sweat and pain catapulted from his face. My mother and I were terrified. But he bossed the knee and never complained.

If he made a decision he would not change his mind no matter how much Mother, I or my sister Margaret pleaded and wheedled. Every misdemeanour was punished with a thwack. His last thwack was when I was eighteen years old, the night before I joined the Royal Navy. I was punished for being ten minutes late home. I never resented the punishments and never stopped loving or respecting Dad. For ninety-nine per cent of the time I perceived the punishments to be fair and just. The same approach failed to work with my sister Margaret. She challenged him, I did not.

My father was acknowledged to be the brightest spark in the Oldham Co-operative Butchery Department and was being groomed to be its Manager when he was conscripted to fight in the Second World War. When he returned five years later the post was filled by Cecil, a non-combatant, and he could only be Deputy. Dad was able and enthusiastic and earned respect. He ran the show and made many important innovations including the novelty of pre-packaging. When Cecil retired, the Board tried to recruit an outside General Manager. Dad was disappointed and furious. He resigned and agreed to buy a business owned by Aunty Ann and her cousin Eleanor. The Coop Board changed their mind; they pleaded and weaselled and offered to buy Dad out of his commitment. But he had given his word and wouldn't change.

We moved into the shop. He made it a success but I always felt he felt he had made a mistake. I loved the shop and my tiny daughters loved their access to the 'penny' sweet tray.

But we didn't have to do the hard and time-consuming work, with so little time for relaxation.

We became very close from the time of his retirement in 1975 until his death, from a third heart attack, in 1993. He never expressed emotions, never complained and continued to scorn adversity or pain. I was surprised to receive a letter after his second attack in October 1988, saying

"....Some warnings are easy to ignore, except in retrospect. The heart attack started with a tightening of the throat; an unusual beating of the pulse; wanting to go to the toilet; an increase in body heat and a feeling of collapse. It's like an unsteady train. You must sit down and close your eyes as the train gets faster and faster. Some of the wheels become square and you bob from side to side. The pain is terrific, every turn of the wheel is more excruciating until you come off the track into a black hole. Round and round. Unbearable. Finally complete silence..............."

He recovered from this setback and continued with his energetic lifestyle for another five years.

My only sister was Margaret Ann (17 July 1943 – 6 July 1998). She died after suffering from Cerebella Ataxia though the actual cause of death was choking on a biscuit crumb in the night. It must have been vile and horrible. She dialled the automatic number on my mobile phone whilst choking, and left a message of despair.

She had three great sporting sons: Simon, Matthew and Danny. She and her wonderful guide dog Jamie were looked after by her deeply caring middle son Matthew and his wife Debbie. She had been deserted by her husband Vincent Jones who was unable to cope with her deteriorating physical condition, though she remained enormously brave, fun loving and beautiful.

The gap between myself and my sister was seven years. This meant I was leaving each phase of my young life when she was joining.

She always had tremendous guts and spirit and would not put up with Dad's unilateral decisions. They had many confrontations when I was in the Navy. Dad had been significantly 'retrained' when I came home and Margaret had completed his retraining by the time we returned from Nigeria. He became a more gentle and sensitive man and a super grandad. This is the man my own daughters will remember.

Margaret and I had lots of chats whilst she was ill with ataxia. I was amazed by how much she knew about me, my inner self, and my ups and downs. I think she had probably idolised her 'big brother' but she knew all my weaknesses, fallibilities and equivocations – things I thought were hidden.

Margaret and my daughter Josephine have many attitudes, emotions and inflexions in common. I dearly love them both and can sometimes daydream them into a single personality.

MY GRANDPARENTS

My maternal grandad, Tom Rhodes (1877 – 1946), was a wonderful person with a good tenor voice who retired as an Inspector of Trams in Oldham. He was a good public speaker and a trade unionist, whom everyone seemed to know. He had one of the country's earliest successful appendix operations, circa 1914, the same year and month as the King. He retired early in the 1930s because of his huge V-shaped scar from neck to navel on paper-thin skin. He spent most of his time indulging me as a child: stories, walking on the moors, running, jumping, making carpentry models, etc. No one told me when he died from a heart attack and I was stunned when I realised, very slowly, weeks later, that the man I loved so dearly was dead. My family didn't involve children in unpleasant things. I would have been ten years old but vividly remember him today. He was very special, very very special in my life.

My grandma, Tamar Rhodes (1878 – 1964), had started work in a cotton mill when she was ten years old. She was a particularly outspoken woman with a very strong character and a wealth of sharp sayings. She was very protective and possessive of her family and it was tough for anyone she crossed. She looked after me a lot after my sister was born in 1943 until I was well into my teens. She also mellowed in old age and died in May 1964 just after my first daughter Josephine was born. She had worked many years as a cotton spinner but told me lots of stories about the Boer War and her favourite brother Samuel who had had his jaw shot away. He had a brass and gold contraption inside his mouth to enable him to eat. Tamar's local mill was often on 'short time' but employees were fiercely loyal and would not take up employment with neighbouring mills only a few hundred metres away, even though there was work to be had and money was desperate. Her great fear had always been the risk of ending her days in 'The Workhouse'.

They lived at 64 Hanson Street, Greenacres, near Greenacres Nursing Home, Oldham where I was born. Two up, two down, no hot water and with gas lighting. A black iron fire range dominated the back room, with an iron oven from which Grandma produced an unending supply of meat pies, fruit pies and wonderful bread. Appendix A provides a more vivid account. Floorboards could be removed in the middle of the room to reveal a perfectly shaped zinc bath, hand filled with water heated on the fire range. I stayed often but never had to bathe. It was for the adults who bathed once a week, in series, on Friday evenings. The outside lavatory had a 'tippler mechanism', connected to all the other lavatories in the street. As the huge tippler gradually filled with waste water, it overbalanced with a thunderous and frightening roar and sluiced a whole street of lavatories.

I particularly liked the enormous flock bed because it precisely moulded to my body shape, providing a haven of warmth in an ice-cold house. I don't think there was a clock in the house although Grandad had a wonderful pendant 'Bobby' watch in his waistcoat which could be opened at several levels. This gift to me was stolen in one of our first burglaries in Croydon. Each morning we were woken by the 'knocker-up' who rat-tat-tatted on the window with a long pole. I have no recollection of the time but I guess it could not have been later than 6.30am. The house had no alarm clocks.

In the early summer of 1943 Tom and Tamar took me for a holiday in Blackpool. We stayed at the bed and breakfast home of my grandma's sister Rachel Newton (nee Sykes), their daughter Evelyn Thompson who was my mother's favourite relation, and Evelyn's three daughters, Irene, Barbara and Margaret. I was just seven years old. I now know my mother was pregnant but didn't then. We travelled early morning by train and bus and I was 'bursting' to get to the beach. I could not contain my excitement. Tom and Tamar indulged me. Straight to the crowded Blackpool beach, off with shirt, shorts and shoes and into the waves ignoring faint calls from behind. I had a wonderful time. I felt hungry for lunch. The crowds seemed to have gone and I looked to the spot near the pier where I had left my grandparents. Nothing, no one. I cried and cried and climbed up onto the promenade. It was hard and cold to my bare feet. I was taken to a police station but didn't know where I was staying or what the people were called. All I could remember was a 34 bus.

A long story... but kind people helped to put me on the bus. I recognised the house, which I had seen for the first time for only ten minutes much earlier in the day. I entered through the kitchen door and found the whole family in tears. They had long decided I had drowned and both lifeboat and coastguard had been out. They had scoured the beach from north to south. We had gone out in the morning at about 11am and it was now 6.50pm in the evening. My grandparents had been hysterical and my grandma retold her horrors until the day she died. My recollection then, and now, is that I had been on the beach only ten or fifteen minutes. In fact I must have been in the waves for five or more hours and walked from North Pier to South Pier without any knowledge of time. Does that happen to children now, I wonder?

My father's mother, Grandma Hannah Humble nee Ward (29 Dec 1882 – 26 July 1952), was always cantankerous when I went on the weekly visit with my father. She was invariably in bed in a downstairs room complaining about everyone and everything. Only later did I learn she had 'taken to her bed' for about ten years. That is what depressed women used to do in those days. There were no drugs. Earlier she had been a very beautiful and extroverted woman who ran the Friendship Inn, Manchester Street, Oldham virtually single-handed after her husband Joseph Edward died from consumption on 8th December 1928. I guess that she had become depressed trying to run the pub on her own in a state of bereavement and devastated at having to relinquish the licence which had been the centre of her family life for as long as she could remember. She lived with her second husband 'Pa', Alfred Hague (born 29 Apr 1885), on Lyndhurst Road in Hollinwood, Oldham opposite Hollins School.

The only likeable thing about my visits was that it gave me access to a wonderful double set of dominoes with brightly coloured numbers. I played number games for hours on the window seat whilst Dad attended to his mother. I am sure it helped my maths.

My father's father, Joseph Edward Humble (1880 – 1928), died of consumption long before I was born. My father said he was always a weakly man who suffered with ill health. My father, then eighteen years old, took him to stay at a guesthouse owned by one of his relations in Blackpool for 'the fresh air'. He never saw him again. His father died a few days later. The first time I saw his photograph was a gift from Aunty Dolly in 2003. It felt very odd to see a picture of my grandfather for the very first time when I was double his age.

GREAT-GRANDPARENTS

I know very little about my maternal great-grandparents except that Tamar's father was George Sykes and he had married Hannah Smethurst. Their children were Tamar (born 1878), Fred, Rachel, Samuel and, youngest, Sarah Alice (Shr'alice). The 'Sykes' were well-known builders who came from Duckinfield and my grandmother Tamar delighted me by saying her father George and her brothers Fred and Sam were builders and had been responsible for the two famous large stone lions and their adjacent steps in Alexandra Park, Oldham. However, I may be mistaken and the builders may have been the 'Rhodes', my grandfather Tom's family.

Tom Rhodes's mother was a Cotteril. His parents had seven children and nineteen grandchildren. Their eldest child was Francis, followed by Sam, Charlie, Thomas (my grandfather), Nellie, Silvia and Fred. I never met any of them because my grandmother Tamar described them as 'boozers'. However, Sam Rhodes's daughter Velma, my mother's cousin, was a local hairdresser and had been one of my mother's two best friends.

I occasionally met Velma's four children: Zena, Jim and twins Ann and Peter Challinor. Jim was three years younger than me and went to Hollins Secondary School. Along with two other pupils he stayed on at sixteen, was awarded three good A levels and went to university – the first time anyone from a secondary school had done so well. There was lots of adulation in the press. Whilst he was at university the Headmaster was sacked because it was found he had deliberately fabricated examination results. However, Jim continued academically and did well. I met him by chance in 1971 at my friend Eric Bolton's house just after Eric appointed him to a top educational job in Croydon. We then lost touch. I imagine he was embarrassed that I knew 'his story', though it was in no way his fault and didn't reflect badly on him at all.

The only branch of the Sykes family – Grandmother Tamar's family – I ever met was her sister Rachel who married Walter Newton. These are the people who had a boarding house in Blackpool and later Runcorn. Their only daughter Evelyn was my mother's other best friend. She married Kenneth Thompson, a senior manager at ICI. Their three lovely daughters, Barbara my age, Irene a year older and Margaret a year younger, always made a great fuss of me when we visited though from seven to seventeen years of age I was embarrassed by girls. I lost touch with their family when I started my national service. I remember my mother being very upset when Evelyn died in the late 1980s.

All Tamar's family were unpopular with my dad. It seems that Mum was always the 'apple of the eye' of her uncle Gerard Booth who married Tamar's youngest sister Sarah Alice (pronounced Sh'ralice). He was a successful businessman and when Mum and Dad were getting married he promised my father a loan if he could find a really good retail business proposition. My parents were excited and delighted, and my father scoured every business in town. My mother said that Dad negotiated a brilliant price for a large newsagent on Lees Road at the bottom of Balfour Street. The money never came; but Uncle Gerard must have thought

Dad had chosen well because, according to my mother, he gave the business to his son, who had been the pageboy at their wedding.

On my father's side, the earliest reference to the Humble family can be found in Southwark Cathedral: a magnificent Flemish sculpture of Alderman Richard Humble (who died 1616) and his two wives Margaret and Isobel.

My great-grandfather John William Humble married Mary Ann Devonport. Their children were John, Joseph Edward (my grandfather, who died in December 1928), Ellen Amelia (who died at the age of two years), Cissie (1882 - 1962), Alfred (died 1946), Frank (died as a baby 1884), Florence and Fred Humble. Mary Ann was a huge bedbound woman over twenty stone whom – my father said – he and his brother Jack used to visit once a week. Their task was to raise her above the bed with block and tackle so that the bedding could be changed.

In the 19th century the Humbles had skin, tripe and violin string works in Newton Heath, North Manchester. In those days it was traditional to leave a business entirely to the eldest brother, who was John, my great-uncle. The expectation was that he would care for the family and the siblings. However, lifelong bachelor John quickly recruited a housemaid, married her and died. The housemaid inherited the house and factory and that was the last the Humble family saw of their quite substantial estate.

The Wards, my grandmother Hannah's family, were quite famous and probably provided our sporting genes. James

Ward, my great-grandfather, was a notable athlete and professional footballer who also won the professional Talbot Bowling Trophy, Blackpool, for which he received the considerable prize of £100. He married Sarah Wright, daughter of William Wright, Chairman of Oldham Brewery. In 1887 James and Sarah became the licensees of the 'Friendship Inn' at 280 Manchester Street, Oldham (not to be confused with a public house of the same name on Lees Road). In 1905 they gave the pub to my grandparents, Joseph Edward Humble and his wife Hannah (nee Ward), their eldest daughter, as a slightly belated wedding present. Joseph and Hannah managed the pub for twenty-five years and this is the place where my father and his siblings were brought up.

James Ward then took over the large Bowling Green Inn, Rochdale and claimed to have sponsored the first international professional tennis and table tennis competitions in the United Kingdom. In 2007 I discovered that the Bowling Green Inn had been demolished but the Friendship Inn, Manchester Street, Oldham was still there. However, the premises were very run-down and it seemed to be one of the few buildings remaining in a quite desolate and depressing part of the town.

Wilkin Ward, one of Hannah's youngest brothers, was regarded as an infamous revolutionary socialist and very much the 'black sheep' of the family. He was involved with his son William in the 'Battle of Blackpool Sands' (to quote a newspaper headline of the time) and a hunger strike up Blackpool Tower. I remember reading about them on the front page of the Daily Herald in 1947 but my branch of the family only referred to them in hushed, conspiratorial tones.

I have recently spoken with son William who became English Communist 'minder' for Paul Robeson on his visits to the UK (Paul Robeson being the world's most famous Negro singer who immortalised 'Old Man River'). In a BBC interview William described waiting in the bedroom alone at the Midland Hotel, Manchester. Paul Robeson was still in the bath, singing. It was 'awesome, magnificent'.

AUNTS AND UNCLES

Aunty Ann and Uncle Fred Rhodes were my godparents. Fred was my mother's only brother, older and very clever at school. They had no children, were relatively wealthy and bought all my extravagances: first long trousers, first tennis racquet, rugby boots, restaurant meals and hotel overnight. They had the first private car I ever saw and certainly the first I sat in. They were always encouraging and seemed to treat me as a contemporary.

Ann, as sharp as a needle, died in 2004 at the age of ninety-three. She was still fit, articulate, popular and pretty but riddled with prejudice: anti-Catholic, anti-Jewish, anti-black, anti-socialist and anti-sex. "I tried it once," she said, "on the first night of my honeymoon. I wasn't going to try it again." I became her only surviving relative and she insisted that in due course I should take her to the crematorium on a wheelbarrow in a plastic bag. I was surprised to discover it would be possible, but more expensive than a conventional ceremony. She arranged instead for her body to be donated to Liverpool University. From her sixties she led an extraordinarily eventful life but not one which is part of this story.

Aunty Ginny (or Jenny), my father's eldest sister, and Uncle Frank (Ainsworth) had three sons, Roy, Neil and Geoffrey, who were all older than me, although Geoffrey and I were in the same class at grammar school. Jenny always seemed straight-laced and holy. I think she took it upon herself to 'instruct' my mother during the Second World War. Frank was very much my father's mentor, adviser and guide. He grew orchids and had the deepest voice I have ever heard. My sister, until the age of about three years, cried every time he spoke. He had a small cellar in the house at No 3 Bath Street, Oldham from which he produced beautiful French-polished, handmade woodwork.

Uncle Fred and Aunty Olga (Humble) were both head teachers. Fred, my father's eldest brother, was Headmaster at Alexander Junior School. He had been an outstanding sportsman and rugby player in his youth and many in Oldham assumed I must be his son. They had one son Malcolm, the same age as my sister, a brilliant academic, who lectured at St Andrew's University. Olga first taught PE and became Deputy Head at a large secondary school in Oldham where Malcolm Boyd, Freda's uncle, was caretaker. Small world. She was a huge woman in later life. They were our neighbours 'on the Coppice' but it was a cold, disciplined house. They were always kind but with little warmth or laughter.

Uncle Jack and Aunty Dorothy (Humble) kept a real fun house. Their son Geoffrey, a few months older than me, was my closest friend. Indeed Jack, two years older than my father, had always been his closest friend. My dad told me, with admiration and affection, of their many 'scrapes'. Jack, top Prudential salesman for year after year, could 'talk the hind legs off a donkey' and frequently did. Dorothy was very warm and beautiful. I loved every visit to their house. She indulged me by always making the most wonderful lemon meringue pie I have ever tasted. It was made with very thick sweet condensed milk.

Aunty Dolly and Uncle Donald (Nuttall). Dolly was twelve years younger than my father and said she idolised him as her favourite brother. I really don't remember much about her until she started courting Donald and they had one daughter, my cousin Jean Lowe. (Jean was a twin but her sister was stillborn.) Dolly says she did a lot of babysitting for me. I don't remember. Donald was very quiet but Dolly a real Ward extrovert, probably like her brother Jack and their mother. She became the catalyst of the Humble family. Brilliant when my sister Margaret was ill and equally keen on my daughters Joey, Becca and Sarah. Dolly died on 27 April 2005.

COUSINS

Roy Ainsworth was godfather to my eldest daughter Josephine. He was eight years older than me and was always kind and generous. He left school to train as a chartered secretary in a cotton mill with his father but lost his job when the cotton industry slumped. He then studied to become an accountant but took several years to qualify. He married lovely Betty who was Private Secretary to Dr Steptoe when he was researching the first test-tube babies. Roy died on 7 September 2007.

Neil Ainsworth was six years older than me. He was enthusiastic and always getting into scrapes. I vividly remember him sobbing during a family visit when I was nine or ten years old. It was because his father insisted he remain the only boy in his school year still wearing short pants. Otherwise he had the widest grin ever seen. We holidayed together in the South of France after I finished national service in 1956 and had a really wonderful time. He pursued every activity with infectious enthusiasm and was a highly respected decorator.

Geoffrey Ainsworth was in my class at grammar school although almost two years older. He originally failed his 11-plus due to hopeless teaching at Freehold Junior School and slipped a year. I was very competitive to try to do better at everything and we were mostly neck and neck in class and at sport, and both generally in the top five in the A stream. He went on to university but had difficulty with a French examination, then essential for a degree. He left to become a highly respected Geography teacher. I liked him at school because he was my cousin but came to like and admire him much more as an adult. He married Joyce Rigby. They have two daughters, Alison and Caroline, who are friends and contemporaries of my daughters.

Geoffrey Humble was my favourite cousin. He was eleven months older but the friend with whom I shared everything. He remains very close and I would do anything to support him. In 2006 he became a great-grandfather. I clearly remember playing 'little bears' behind chairs, when I would be scarcely two years old. I have noticed that my grandchildren James and Ben and later Alice and Thomas played the same games. We often stayed together when we were five to eleven years old and had wonderful weekends at Blackpool with our parents, who were also best friends. We were fiercely competitive. We both used a lot of ingenuity to cheat to win, particularly at Monopoly. His father was in the Air Force during the war and could take his wife and child with him. Geoffrey used to disappear from my life and I remember the ecstasy when he reappeared. He became a self-employed dental mechanic and both he and his wife Margaret retired when he was fifty years old. In November 2004 I took him to Oldham RFC 100th anniversary. He has a heart condition and collapsed. I thought he would not survive. He did, just.

Malcolm Humble (Dr) was born in 1943 and went to school with my sister Margaret. He was an amazing child, close to genius, reading fluently at four years old and devouring adult books by the time he was six. He was always very serious, didn't like to play and gained an early scholarship to Manchester Grammar. Academically brilliant at Cambridge, he became Research Fellow at Emmanuel College, Lecturer in German Literature at St Andrew's University in 1969 and world expert on Brecht. He remained at St Andrew's until he died on 31 May 2006. He appeared to have no small talk or social skills and died intestate. His estate, estimated at £1 million gross, is due to be divided equally between various cousins.

Jean Nuttall is ten years younger than I. I was recruited as the organiser of her parties when in my teens but don't really remember much until her wedding to Ian Lowe. Joey, Becca and Sarah (circa four, three and two years) looked stunning in identical turquoise flowered dresses. Jean and her mother supported my sister Margaret when she became ill with ataxia. I found Jean to be a lovely lovely person. She plays golf quite seriously and is witty and forthright. A biology teacher, she was until recently Deputy Head of Science at Counthill School. She seems to admire Freda and is one of the most welcome family visitors to our home.

EARLY FRIENDS

Werneth Crescent Gang. Until the age of twelve or thirteen I spent every spare holiday, summer evening and weekend playing out, either on Werneth Crescent for football and cricket, as there were no cars to interfere, or alternatively on Blackie's Field, now the site of Grange Avenue School. It was here where we hid and chased, lit bonfires, played Rallyho and Duckie, fell in the pond and got up to all kinds of adolescent mischief in some partly built houses. (Building had stopped in 1939 because of the War.) I would call for any of the following to 'come out to play': Stuart Woodhead, Derek Hulme, Donnie Taylor, Billy Ross, Alan Fisher or John Fletcher, and occasionally girls: Pam Hoyland, Pat Eglin and Pat Farimond.

We were an independent group and never played with the Lacrosse Avenue Gang or the Little African Gang although those children lived less than two hundred yards away. I lost touch with everyone except Stuart Woodhead. Donnie Taylor became a journalist on the Oldham Chronicle and wrote the newspaper article on my daughter Sarah nearly being gassed as a baby. Pam Hoyland became a TV glamour girl on an old Granada quiz programme and married a GP. Alan Fisher bought a large petrol station.

Stuart Woodhead. I have been in touch with Stuart throughout the whole of my life although I doubt we have ever had much of a conversation until recently. We met, said his mother, when they moved into No 4 Werneth Crescent on his third birthday. (He's still there.) The removal van left and a little boy knocked on the door (me) and said, "Have you got a little boy I can play with?" From that moment we played the same sports and games and went to the same infants' school, junior school and grammar school together. He has sent a Christmas card every year, but until recently it never said more than "from Stuart".

He struggled at Counthill Grammar School and never seemed outstanding at sports. We went everywhere together and when I left Oldham to play professional rugby he went to Manchester RUFC. He finished by getting seventeen caps for Lancashire and became a single figure golfer. He lives in the same house and has never married and I am unaware of other friends. I always try to see him when I visit Oldham. We had our first good chat for years at the recent Rugby Union centenary and it didn't seem sixty-five plus years since we first met. I saw much more of Stuart in 2007 after he was identified with lymphatic cancer. He has my respect.

I liked all my friends (1943 to 1950) except John Fletcher. He was taller and three years older than me and, at the time, a nasty vicious bully. He once split open my head with a steel spade, and several times I came home crying with deep scratches on my face. I really hated him though I don't remember being scared. I just became obsessed and determined to 'get my own back' when my size caught up to his. It did, when I was home on leave from the Navy aged nineteen. I saw him at the Savoy Dance Hall in Oldham and realised he seemed weakly and gangling. He looked, and probably was, a fragile creature. My angst immediately expired. I just said "Hello" and "Where are you working?" I have never hated or seriously disliked any individual since.

EARLY MEMORIES.

My first memory is of being in a pram with a cat net over the top and feeling the warm rain, my mother pushing the pram and saying to someone, possibly her mother, "I'll see you on Tuesday." I have always had a vivid impression of that event which I subsequently discussed with my mother. We worked out I was less than two years old.

As I small child I remember seeming to spend many hours on the potty having very difficult or impossible bowel movements. I remember my mother consulting neighbours about the possibility of 'an operation'. The inconvenience caused no further problems until I was diagnosed with prostate cancer in 2003. A consultant said he was amazed I had never had to have an operation to slacken a very strong anal muscle. Is this hereditary?

One hereditary quirk we have already identified is a slightly malformed middle toe on my left foot. For several early years I had to attend a special clinic spending ages trying to pick up a pencil with my toes. Very boring. However, it did the job. My daughter Rebecca was born with a similar toe and we have spotted an analogous anomaly on new baby Elliot.

Still pre-school pre-war, I have many memories of playing with cousin Geoffrey Humble, particularly being at their huge, rented but dangerous house 'Austen Longs' at Waterhead: playing with melted road tar in the garden and trying to block ant (or mouse) holes. The house seemed to have a great ballroom and grand piano. I would like to revisit it as it still stands proudly above Oldham. I clearly remember a great fuss when they had to move out and subsequently discovered this was early in the War when I was just four years old. Jack Humble had leased the house "to show off" said my hostile opinionated grandmother Tamar.

I clearly remember my first day at school. I remember a large classroom on the left of the front door and a confusing and chaotic crowd of children and mothers. It seemed very threatening. I remember the fear, dread and absolute panic when my mother left me in the classroom with strangers. I sobbed and sobbed in a quite uncontrolled manner. I couldn't stop. I remember being given a crayon to draw with. A neighbour tried to soothe me. It was Stuart's mother, trying to reassure me by saying, "Stuart's here. Sit next to him." I did and he (Stuart Woodhead) has remained a lifelong friend.

My other strong first-year school memory was sitting on a very low outside window ledge in the playground at Werneth School. In our first year the playground seemed enormous and at playtime I rushed to be first to sit on the corner of this window ledge facing the school gates. Is it still there? A regular companion was a very tall girl called Margaret Callaghan. I remember being dazzled looking at long hairs on her forearms, illuminated by the sun. I imagined I could walk between them. Later I was embarrassed by my family. One of my aunts, probably Dorothy, asked whether I had a girlfriend at school. I said, "Yes, I love Margaret Callaghan." They asked, "Why?" I said, "Because she has golden hairs on her arms." I can still hear their hysterical laughter. It helped teach me to think before I spoke... a characteristic I have tried to maintain.

The playground was never entirely 'safe'. We shrank away from the Second Years and never crossed the invisible demarcation line between the Infants' and Junior Schools. We played competitive games with marbles but no one wanted to lose their most treasured possessions: losers trying to regain their losses was the cause of squabbles and fights. From time to time girls gathered like a flock of starlings to chase and catch a boy to kiss. I was petrified of being caught.

I have no recollection of classroom work in the Infants' but do remember the Hall. We seemed to do a lot of dancing practice around the maypole and had visits from a peripatetic music teacher who arrived with dozens of triangles and tambourines. There was a cacophony of noise.

I lived at the very bottom of Wellington Road – no 208 - and always went home for lunch. There was plenty of time as the school broke from 12 noon until 1.45 hours. School dinners were introduced circa 1943. My mother persuaded me to give them a trial. The meat course was cold and consisted of gristle. This was followed by a milk pudding. It was either sago or tapioca but the more confident children said, "It's frogspawn with milk on." My stomach did somersaults. I was horrified. I never stayed for school dinner again and I've never eaten milk puddings until this day.

At home we had rabbits and my favourite was Domino. They used to disappear from time to time and I was six or seven before I realised my father used to kill them, by hand, for dinner. He built a magnificent high swing across the path that was the absolute envy of the Werneth Crescent gang. Good for my ego because, except for Stuart, all the others were two or three years older.

On Mondays, between the ages of three and five, I used to go with my mother to the steam filled wash-house on Heron Street and sit in the basket whilst Mother battered the clothes on a metal scrubbing board in big lead troughs. The clothes were later pressed/dried through large automatic rollers. I hated the smell of chemicals and the heat and the boredom. I remember being scared 'cos I was threatened with being put between the rollers if I misbehaved. One boy did put his hand on the rollers and had to have it amputated. Very dangerous.

The wash-house reminds me of a distressing family trauma. My sister Margaret was home from school with an infection. Mother was at the wash-house leaving Grandma Tamar in charge. She was teaching my sister to crochet a wool snake through the hole of an empty cotton reel. If the wool tangled it needed to be separated by a sharp pointed implement. Grandma unpicked with my Mother's razor-pointed tailoring scissors which she then left in the bedroom. Margaret, aged six years, tried to separate a tangle alone but jabbed the scissors into the centre of her right eye. I arrived for lunch. Grandma was in meltdown and mother, just back from the wash-house, was rushing for help. The GP was brilliant. He drove Margaret to the distant Manchester Eye Hospital. The surgeons managed to stitch between the iris and the pupil. Her sight was saved but most of the bright blue iris was permanently lost. It gave her a disconcerting, though not unattractive appearance. However I shuddered when my daughters used scissors and continue to shudder when I see them used by my grandchildren. Fortunately, the blunt-ended scissors of today are so much safer than the vicious instruments of my youth.

I don't remember anything about the start of the Second World War though I do remember, when I was four or five years old, a barrage balloon appearing above the house. One of the support cables was anchored alongside our back gate. The cable was very thick and just disappeared into the clouds, or smog. I fantasised it was something to do with Jack and the Beanstalk. There was great excitement if a bomb dropped nearby. I don't ever remember hearing a bomb but I do remember hunting in the garden and surrounding streets for pieces of shrapnel. It was brilliant if we found a fresh piece still hot from the explosion.

We had an Anderson bomb shelter in the garden. I helped my father surround it with bags of sand before he went to Australia. The aim was to insulate the shelter against bomb blasts. At one period of the War, air raid warnings sounded almost every night and my mother carried me out in the cold night air into the shelter lit by candles. The smell was very distinctive. I can smell it now! The walls dripped with condensation. If I was awake we made shadow pictures on the wall or a neighbour might drop in and tell ghost stories. I was probably seven or eight years old.

In 1943, when I was seven, my sister Margaret was born. I had no idea where babies came from or that my mother was pregnant although I do remember being asked for my favourite names. I chose 'Margaret'. I think I was still infatuated with Margaret Callaghan although I had never spoken to her or looked at her since my first days in the Infants'. We were playing cricket in the street when an ambulance stopped at my house. Horror! I saw my mother taken into the rear. It set off and I chased and chased until I fell hard and my knees were torn and full of gravel. A neighbour, Alice Knowles, took me in and spent what seemed hours picking gravel out of my knees with a needle. She also explained about babies. I thought they were found under mulberry bushes. The birth information seemed bizarre and I still have the scars on my knees to remind me of my astonishment.

Early in 1943 my father was conscripted into the Navy but was allowed six weeks' leave to help my mother and the new baby. I saw rather more of him than I had ever seen before and remember him cooking meals, usually sausages in cloying melted cheese. He took me to my first football match, at Oldham Latics. My father had not made a big impression to date. Retailers worked long hours and I guess he was mostly at work when I was awake. However, he was very strict and quick to slap hard, very hard. I learned never to demand or dissent and to be wary. When his leave was over he knew he would be sent overseas and also knew the mail was censored. No one could reveal locations. He and I devised an elaborate code with the names of imaginary aunts and uncles each meaning a different country or part of the world.

It was like being Dick Barton (an early James Bond). Several weeks later a letter arrived and mentioned the health of

Aunty 'Amelia'... and we knew he was on his way to Australia. It was so thrilling to have such a secret. I told no one except my mother.

I always felt loved and confident. But any deficiency in demonstrable affection was compensated for by Grandad Tom Rhodes. Until I had a wife and children of my own I loved him more than everyone else in my world.

He achieved fame, or notoriety, by being the only manager who supported 'the men' in a major strike circa 1928. Everyone we met admired him. His time was at my absolute disposal. Every bus and tram would stop to pick him up en route for our walks into Oldham or walks on the moors to Pots and Pans or Indians Head, collecting blackberries, making rush whips, climbing rocks, paddling in streams, and finishing each day timing greyhounds or whippets at the local racetrack with his massive stopwatch. Often we played crown green bowls in Watersheddings Park. I was a very respectable partner and the two of us could easily beat most OAPs.

When Grandma Tamar was out shopping, we could do anything at his home at 64 Hanson Street: catching and striking coins with tennis balls, climbing in the eaves, clay pipes with bubbles over the rugs, flooding the yard and making the tippler lavatory thunder, hammering and sawing ingenious models. I once accidentally sawed through the arm of their best rocking chair and didn't get the slightest censure. When Tamar saw the damage she was furious: I shook. Grandad said it had been entirely done by him and he would soon get a new arm and repair the chair.

But best of all was his game of 'Spring-Heeled Jack'. They had three well-sprung easy chairs plus a settee which he put in a line from the front parlour, through the vestibule and out into the street. I ran from across the road, cheered by male neighbours, and bounced over the backs from chair to chair at ever increasing distances. When the wives were out other sprung chairs were brought by the man next door. It was fantastic, absolutely 'wicked', and we were never rumbled...

I so looked forward to seeing him at weekends and school holidays. I have already explained no one told me when he died. It seemed weeks before I slowly realised what had happened. He was never mentioned in my hearing and for years I thought I caught a glimpse of him in a crowd or waiting for me at a street corner. I was very sad.

JUNIOR SCHOOL

My school days were always happy and I guess I was a bright and popular boy. However, I was very worried about moving from the security of the Infants' School to the Juniors. Our ears were filled with stories of 'rites of passage'. Our heads were going to be flushed down the lavatories on our first day. We would be beaten by sticks. I got stubborn and point-blank wouldn't go to school. I was clearly frightened and my mother sought the help of one of the teachers who lived close by. He (Mr Taylor?) gave assurances that the stories were untrue and he would take charge. There were never any problems although I think we repeated the threats, the following year, to the next class of children. Horrid.

We arrived at school one Monday morning to find to our astonishment all the iron railings and gates around the school had disappeared. "It's for the war," said the Headmaster 'Pop' Loader. "It is to fight Hitler." I just couldn't imagine what he meant. Surely it wasn't possible to hit Hitler with a school railing as though it was a spear? We were all confused. Steeped in stories about Cowboys and Indians and Zulu warriors, some of us wondered whether the railings, like spears, were to be thrown from aeroplanes! Then air raid shelters appeared parallel to the cricket ground wall. I have no recollection of going inside the shelters although the sand and soil piled on top of them made a wonderful mountain range from which to attack the enemy. Whosoever that enemy might be.

The only other impact of the war at school was 'gas mask practice'. Hateful. These were some of the very worst moments at school. We had to put on thick rubber gas masks once a week and practise for what seemed longer and longer periods. They were suffocatingly horrible. It made me heave and choke. If I thought no one was watching, my eyes watering, I would insert my fingers under my chin into the rubber to catch a breath of fresh air.

Our teacher was Miss Willock in both the second and third of the four years at junior school. She was kind, gentle and lovely. This is where the focus was on reading and writing. Reading seemed to involve massively boring books about 'Old Lob'. Writing was repeating time and time again the same letter for page after page, e.g. aaaaaaaaaaaaaaaaaa or bbbbbbbbbbbbbbbbbb etc. I remember one unfairness. My father was serving in the Royal Navy in Australia. He sent a parcel which included some coral and some bananas. No one had ever seen a banana and Miss Willock asked me to bring them to school. I did. They were rock hard and jet black. The unfairness was that Miss Willock asked me to spell the word 'banana'. Horrors. I was reluctant to bring things again.

In the third year I was School Leader of Red House. My three fellow leaders and I spent Friday afternoons visiting every classroom to collect and total 'good' points awarded to each house during the week. At the end of the year Red House won by a landslide and I was terrified at having to make a speech to all the school on the last day of term. I know I practised and practised. But even days later I couldn't recollect what I said or what had happened. The fear blocked everything out. Ironic in that 'making speeches' became a major feature of my professional life.

This was 1945, the year that the Second World War ended. We were told very little about the War whilst at school. Perhaps we were being insulated against the horrors. I have already mentioned VE Day (Victory in Europe which fell on my birthday – the day I walked home from school to find my house and the neighbours' houses bedecked with bunting), but VJ Day, Victory in Japan, was three months later when the USA dropped an atom bomb on Hiroshima. The people who lived on Werneth Crescent had had time to organise a fabulous street party. My mother made me a wonderful Robin Hood costume out of bits and bats and in the evening, in the dark, there was a singsong. I had established a reputation as a choirboy and was pressed to sing a solo. I was excruciatingly embarrassed but sang 'Jerusalem'. By the time I got to 'Bring Me My Bow of Burning Gold...' I noticed almost all of the adults were crying, with one or two sobbing noisily. It gave me a strangely disturbed feeling. A funny sense of power.

When I was nine or ten years old it was decided I should learn the piano – a gift from Uncle Fred and Aunty Ann to impress my father when he came home from the War. My tutor was the elderly Mr Wright, my father's uncle, the organist at St Margaret's Church. This was followed by eight years of purgatory, as I had to undertake one full hour's practice each day, time I thought I could have better spent playing out with my friends and later at football and cricket practice. I hated the solitary nature of piano practice, so I was thrilled when Freda encouraged each of our daughters to learn an orchestral instrument and be part of a musical community. I could play from sheet music but was never able to improvise. My party pieces from memory were the Warsaw Concerto, Glass Mountain and Hungarian Rhapsodies. I loved to pound out the dramatic chords and was able to perform tolerably well into my forties. I can now play little more than the opening phrases.

My music lessons did have a cultural side effect. Mr Wright was rarely ready to give my lesson at the appointed time and I often had to wait a long long time in his musty library. I had been an avid young reader of boys' school and Biggles adventures, but nothing more challenging. Whilst waiting for my music lessons I read, or started, HG Wells' 'Invisible Man', George Orwell's 'Animal Farm' and Aldous Huxley's 'Brave New World'. I was absolutely riveted. Many of the descriptions and issues remain powerfully in my mind.

In the 4th Year, for 11-plus, we did nothing but IQ test after IQ test. Occasionally we wrote a story such as 'My Life as a Ball' or 'A Cat' or 'A Bicycle'. I enjoyed all the competitive IQ testing – and still do – I thought I was quite good - but do not recall learning anything about other countries, history, reading or much arithmetic. I discovered much later that the teacher, Mr Harold Bailey, used every ounce of his energy to get us to grammar school and extend our life opportunities. To him nothing else mattered. He succeeded. Almost every pupil in the class got to grammar school, to East Oldham High School or Hulme Grammar. I was top boy in Oldham. My mother was very proud. My cousin Geoffrey was top boy in the A stream at the neighbouring school Freehold where scarcely any pupil got to grammar school.

In the 4th Year I was made Captain of the School Cricket Team, an appointment which was embarrassing and thoroughly undeserved. There were better cricketers than me such as Terry Cooper and Brian Ogden. However we easily won every match we played and the East Lancashire Junior School Cup by an enormous margin. We always aimed to bat first (other teams chose to bat second) and could suspend our innings at 30 runs rarely having lost more than two or three wickets. We then skittled out most other school teams for an average total of ten runs. Werneth was the undisputed champion. This was the first activity to stimulate my sporting confidence.

GRAMMAR SCHOOL

We eleven-year-olds were terrified in the weeks before going to grammar school. We were again told (by older boys) that we would have to endure an ordeal such as 'head down the lavatory', being beaten or being thrown in a pit in the school basement surrounded by rails. I was much relieved when I discovered my father's allocated holiday coincided with my first two weeks at grammar school. We went to Scarborough and I had my first girlfriend whom I thought of as my sweetheart. We walked the prom together and I was desolate when the holiday finished.

However, missing the first week of school had an unfortunate consequence which has amused my family for years. It was French lessons. At eleven years of age I really didn't understand people spoke different languages in different parts of the world. I thought, at best, they were substitution IQ codes for English, letter by letter. I considered myself very sharp at codes and couldn't see why we were wasting time learning whole 'French' words. I ignored the teaching and just waited for the master codes to be revealed. Everything would become transparent. How long I waited I don't know… a week?.. two weeks?.. five lessons? But I do remember the mind-numbing shock I felt when I realised there was no code and that the whole language was different. It's a failing from which I never recovered. French was always my poorest subject. And I was supposed to be the brightest boy of the year. Perhaps it was the downside of 'Pop' Bailey's concentration on the 11-plus.

Apart from languages I was bright at school, in the A stream, and usually top in Maths and Art and within the top two or three in Geography and History, about middle in Science and English, but near the bottom in French (and later German). Every subject was carefully graded. The positions in class were very important. Terry Cooper, my cousin Geoffrey Ainsworth and I seemed to be 2, 3 or 4 in any order with Russell Lumb always top. I rated it a success only when I beat Geoffrey. I am sure he did not have the same foolish thoughts.

I don't remember any particular sporting achievements in the first two years. In my third year I had a rupture after falling off my bicycle and had an operation at the Oldham Royal Infirmary. I seemed to be off school for a long time and on the day I returned I collapsed. Eventually I made my way home and remember a horribly long walk, with my mother, to the doctor across Oldham. He diagnosed chronic appendicitis and an hour later I was back in the Victorian Oldham Infirmary for another operation. I don't remember much about the operation but do remember having a hateful enema and having to drink foul 'pigeon's milk' prior to the anaesthetic. Also the ribald comments of the older men patients. It was a men's ward; I was thirteen and understood nothing of the rude and puzzling innuendo.

After two months' absence I returned to school for exams. My mother helped enormously by hearing me recite from the various books and notes. She patiently listened for hours and hours. It was something she continued to do right through to my O levels and later my professional examinations. It must have been tediously boring for her.

However, in that exam I felt ashamed to have finished 10th and found it difficult to understand why my mother was delighted. She even gave me extra money to spend on comics. Only later did I understand when I heard her boasting to a friend that I had done well despite missing most of the academic year.

My sporting ability did not reveal itself until the 4th Year. It was September 1950. I played, in a very undistinguished way, in the trials for the under-15s soccer team. When we finished I waited, still in my football boots, for Stuart Woodhead who had chosen to play in the rugby trials. The sports master saw me on the touchline and told me to join in. It was so amazingly easy. If someone had the ball then just tackle hard around the knees. If someone passed the ball then run like the wind to score a try. In the trial I did it repeatedly. From that moment I never again played soccer. Rugby was my sport.

Also by the end of that year I had done well at athletics. I had no stamina to run long distances, even 440 yards seemed like a marathon, but I was fastest over 100 yards and the hurdles, and the best long jumper, high jumper and triple jumper in the school. I long-jumped for Lancashire and was Middle School Sports Champion. I still have my first newspaper cutting. I felt very proud. Both my Uncle Freds (Rhodes and Humble) took a keen interest in my burgeoning prowess but I remember really wishing my grandad could have been there, to see the fruits of his 'Spring-Heeled Jack'. I thought of him fondly then and at key times in my life and continue to think of him now.

In the 5th Form we moved from our dilapidated East Oldham High School in the middle of town to the brand new Counthill Grammar School, high on the Pennines above Oldham. We were encouraged to work hard for our O levels but my main memory was the sunshine and the fact that for most of the year Oldham below was invisible. It was cloaked by a veil of thick black smog. After leaving school we travelled down to a smoke- and smog-ridden pit. In those days some 300 factories belched smoke from enormously tall chimneys. It must have taken some toll on our lungs.

The other issue of the time was to decide a career. Both my parents wanted me to be a teacher. I didn't, principally because I didn't want to be like my teacher relations Uncle Fred and Aunty Olga. My Geography mistress Annie Platt, who had her 100th birthday a few years ago, took me under her wing and said that as I was so good at Maths and Art I ought to aim for architecture. Surveying was another career she had in mind. Fate had another plan.

WORKING HOLIDAYS

I never recall having pocket money from my parents but had to negotiate money for every specific thing from my father: for a bus fare, the cinema, a comic or the speedway at Bellevue. I can still smell the Bellevue Manchester cinder track although it is more than fifty years ago. Mother would give me money if she could, but times must have been hard. Grandma Rhodes would give me something on pension day and Aunty Ann would lend me pennies to gamble with her at cards, and then let me win.

To try to supplement my income I got various jobs in the school holidays. My cousin Geoffrey Ainsworth and I twice worked at the Nile Mill, where his father was Company Secretary, and pushed skips of empty cotton reels to the spinners for about 18 shillings per week. Another holiday we cleaned company cars for an engineering company and once Uncle Fred arranged for me to work in the office at Dronsfield Brothers. Although I got 25 shillings a week I hated the office job and knew that that wouldn't be my career.

In June 1952, after I had finished my O Levels, Grandma Rhodes produced an Oldham Chronicle with an advert for a Trainee Weights and Measures Inspector. I didn't know what it was, neither did my parents. But everyone seemed to think it was secure and respectable. I went for the job in the belief that I might do it for the duration of the school holidays and get a bit more money than in an office, a garage or a cotton mill. I was interviewed by a very charming police superintendent: Dick Butler, who was also Chief Weights and Measures Inspector, Oldham. I didn't learn much about the job but remember being very flattered to be treated seriously. I then left for a camping holiday in Brixham, Devon with ten schoolmates, the sports master Fred Llewellyn, his wife and five-year-old son.

This was my first holiday without my parents and we had a wonderful sporty time. The ten of us slept in one huge military bell tent. In the last week, in 1952, the centre pole snapped on the night of the infamous Lynton and Lynmouth floods. We took half-hour shifts to support the pole through the night. At dawn we found the campsite was totally devastated with other tents and caravans having blown over the cliffs. That was the end of a super holiday and I returned home to find I'd been offered the job in Weights and Measures on 35 shillings a week.

Monday 9 August 1952 was my first day at work. My secret plan was to stay for a month and then return to school to take A levels. I was allocated to one of the inspectors, Jack Stainthorpe, who said he would collect me at 5am the second morning. He wanted to trail a fraudulent coal dealer from the Coal Depot in Manchester to the houses where he was due to deliver coal in Oldham.

I was just sixteen years of age. It was exciting being up and out so early, lying in wait in Manchester and following unseen a rogue coal dealer called George Pickford. Normally householders had five or ten bags but he was delivering some fours and nines and one eight. "We have caught him cold," said Jack. And we had, as the court case three months later conclusively proved. But I was thrilled. It was the job I wanted and I couldn't, at that stage, have anticipated anything better. I never went back to school and some of my ten holiday friends I never saw from that day to this.

YOUTHFUL MISCELLANY

The lessons at grammar school were mostly very boring. I guess that, after the 1939-1945 War, the teaching was poor. Lessons, except Art and Maths, consisted of a teacher dictating notes which we furiously copied and then learnt parrot-style for tests and exams. I had no difficulty memorising the notes but I don't claim much understanding. I found Physics and Mechanics mystifying and did not attempt the O level exam. However, the year after leaving school I had to pass the subject for my profession. I read once through one textbook and everything slotted into place like magic. The confusions of five years disappeared and I scored circa 90%. Modern education is so much more enlightened.

From about eight years to fifteen years we played out when not at school. I've already mentioned our Werneth Crescent gang and we were out and about every night, weekends and holidays. The year's biggest event was preparing for a huge November 5th bonfire on Mother Blackjack's Field. We spent the greater part of the summer holidays scouring gardens and copses for wood and trees and visited every local cotton mill asking for old cotton skips. The height of the bonfire was immense but I remember the fear when the older boys put Stuart Woodhead and me, the youngest, under an inverted skip. They sometimes kept us trapped for hours. Our more sadistic 'friends' poked sticks through the wicker gaps. We never squealed or complained.

The main games were Rallyho or Duckie or Peggy. The first two invariably involved one team hunting another on all the surrounding streets. Rallyho was suitable for an area covering several streets and one team were given a count of a hundred to go and hide. Duckie was in a smaller copse or bomb-site and one person erected a column of twelve to fifteen half bricks which the others had to knock down before they ran to hide and the searcher had to rebuild before looking. One hunt could easily last half a day and my only problem was getting home on time. I didn't have a watch but was expected to be exactly on time. It was always the last second and I was always in trouble.

Peggy was different, in that a peg was put on a half brick, flipped in the air and hit as far as possible. The opposition then estimated the highest number of strides the hitter would be able to take and still not reach the peg. If he managed it, he scored the runs but if he did not, then the opposition scored. I loved the game because I think I could leap very long distances, much further than the opposition usually estimated. It's probably why I became so good at triple jumping. In family records there is a lovely picture of my father-in-law Cllr Fred Holden in his mayoral robes hitting off at the 1961 Oldham Peggy competition.

As we grew older the games changed to football and cricket which were played on the street at the side of our house. We were rarely troubled by cars. Very different today. I certainly had sporting talent but at no stage of my life did I have skill training for any sport. That is also very different from the highly focussed pressure training of young people today.

Most of our toys were home-made. We made whips to spin tops, catapults to shoot stones. Very dangerous. I remember Alan Fisher being hit in the eye and no end of broken greenhouse windows. We never confessed. My favourite was the bow and arrow. Earlier Grandad Rhodes had shown me the strongest and most springy tree branches to use for the bow and how to mould street tar to weight the arrowheads. We had lots of distance and accuracy competitions.

When I was thirteen or fourteen years old my parents decided that my sister Margaret needed a bedroom of her own and we moved from our two-bedroomed house at 208 Wellington Road (at the corner of Werneth Crescent) to a three-bedroomed house at 35 Oriel Avenue. It wasn't too far distant but it seemed like the other side of the world. I was unhappy at the loss of my friends. Initially I returned to Werneth Crescent to play but gradually took up with another group who played in Copster Park. We also started to play tennis. Nanny (Freda) and her sister Shirley were part of that group. Although we didn't have any conversations I knew they were special and was most impressed when Freda, although it might have been Shirley, offered to lend me her much superior tennis racquet.

The following year I went out in a foursome with Ian Simpson and the two 'free love' Holden sisters. I, in common with the other fifteen-year-old boys, had not the slightest idea what 'free love' meant. To us it meant we could always go freely to their house at 24 Meadow Lane and meet their lovely mother who would talk to us about life and our aspirations. Nancy Holden was a revelation because she didn't treat children like children. She was interested in our views. Aunty Ann Rhodes was the only other adult who ever did this. Indeed, my aunt continued to treat me as a mature adult and share her confidences and bizarre experiences throughout the whole of her long life. I guess her warmth and kindness to me mitigated, or minimised in my mind, her many bigotries and more outlandish statements. (See page 30.) I certainly did not share her views but neither did I constantly try to correct her.

ST JOHN'S CHURCH

The other centre of my social life was St John's Church, Werneth. I remember a hot dusty claustrophobic Sunday afternoon, early 1945, when 'The Gang' had strung Stuart upside down from the top of a lamppost. I think we may have been trying to re-enact the death scene of Benito Mussolini, the Italian fascist leader who supported Hitler. Stuart was howling when Aunty Jenny Ainsworth came on the scene and made us let him down. She then berated my mother for letting me run wild. My father (Aunty's youngest brother) was still in Australia in the Navy. She insisted that I more regularly attend groups at St John's Church. I did: the Sunday School, the cubs, the scouts, the youth club - where I learned to play table tennis very well – various pantomimes and concerts.

When I got older there was snooker, old-time dancing and whist drives almost every other Saturday night. I was a choirboy, soloist and an altar boy, called 'server'. Indeed I remained a church server until I was twenty-two years old though I don't remember, ever, having any significant feelings on spirituality. We used to play card games in the pews, for money, out of sight of the congregation and the Vicar.

It was exactly a one-mile walk from my house to the church and I walked or ran the distance on average eight times a week for about seven years, sometimes three times on Sundays. They were very happy times and we were always doing something active. In 2001 I visited Oldham and looked up an old St John's friend, Margaret Lamb. We had last met about fifty years earlier but had a brilliant exchange of memories. Her husband, my friend Newty Nield, had died but, astonishingly, I discovered she still met up with our old St John's crowd every Saturday night. Most of them had never moved, had married within the group, never left that part of Oldham and had remained close friends with few outsiders.

Whilst my life seems to have changed and changed and changed again, theirs remains a 'fly in amber'. Surprisingly moving and very nostalgic.

COLTS RUGBY

I was an okay rugby player at school but nothing special perhaps because I was a 5th Former playing in a team of Upper and Lower 6ths, i.e. up to three years older. However, when I left school I joined Oldham Rugby Union Club at Keb Lane. It was an under-18s side and the first match was against Counthill Grammar School including cousin Geoffrey who had stayed into the 6th Form. I'd been made Colts Captain. I couldn't wait for the game and so much wanted to thrash them. I remember sidestepping through their team in the first few minutes when a call came from the touchline that I should come off and join the A Team who were one man short.

In those days Keb Lane had six teams and a Colts side. I did not want to leave and was bitterly, bitterly disappointed when the game was stopped (by the club official refereeing) until I joined the adjacent pitch to play with a lot of fat old men on the A Team. I hated it. But must have done well because the next week I was selected for the 1st Team and I never played Colts rugby or Second Team rugby again. It was September 1952. I was sixteen years old and still two years away from my first shave.

WORK and CAREER

I was enjoying my job. It was interesting. I was out in the fresh air, doing routine inspections in shops, factories and pubs – trying to catch cheats. They were mainly dishonest coalmen, market traders who used false weights or put elastic bands under their scales, and poor bakers who had overcooked their bread and made it short weight. I was trainee to two inspectors: David Pryde and Jack Stainthorpe. Jack later became my best man. Looking back, I am amazed that almost every time we caught a cheat he confessed and said, "It's a fair cop, guv." This was the mid 50s but by the end of the 60s it never happened.

I went to night school in Manchester at Ducie Avenue (now a college of Manchester University) and studied hard to pass the Intermediate stage of my professional examination. Prostitutes worked from doorways in the short stretch of Ducie Avenue to the main Oxford Road. We students were terrified and always waited in the bright lights until we had a group of five or six to scurry eyes down past their bawdy comments.

Every male had to do two years' military service. On my 18th birthday, having just had successful Intermediate exam results, I had to decide whether to apply for national service or seek deferment. Prevailing wisdom was that it was best to 'get it over with'. More than ninety-nine per cent of young men did their national service in the army or the air force but I thought to be different. On Jack Stainthorpe's advice I applied to join the Navy. I was coached to say I played rugby for Oldham's 1st team and had wanted to follow my father's footsteps. Everyone was astonished when I was accepted. I reported to Portsmouth Naval Base within a month on 9 August 1954. I was given a number DM 940373, which I can never forget. I have also never forgotten my Coop 'divvy' number 16294 which I must have last uttered fifty-seven years ago.

It was awful leaving home. My parents both came to Piccadilly Station in Manchester to see me off, but what upset me most was to see my father's eyes full of tears. Until that stage of my life he had always been tough and strict, a very stern disciplinarian. I had often been whacked for any failure or indiscretion, including the night before I left home. The punishment was because I arrived home at 10.40 hours instead of the deadline of 10.30. I was therefore disoriented the following morning to see him upset. Much later I discovered the previous night's punishment had caused quite a furore in the family, my grandma, mother and Aunty Ann telling him he should have been ashamed. However, I didn't resent it as I got away with far more than I was punished for.

Many years later my father told me he had hit me that night not because he was angry but because he was so upset that I hadn't spent my last night with Mum and Dad. I was punished often and usually hit with a single blow, very hard, about the head. I saw stars but it did not occur to me that the punishment might have been unfair or unjust. Conversely, as I have said, my father's attempts to discipline my sister never worked. She always objected and vigorously challenged his authoritarian decisions. That kind of confrontation was absent from my relationship with him.

NATIONAL SERVICE

I reported to the Naval Barracks in Portsmouth (HMS Victory) for six weeks' basic training. I was in a mess with about forty recruits only six of whom were national service. The mess (where we slept) was rife with cockroaches, which we discovered when we found our boots full of them next morning. We were issued with one enamelled plate and one enamelled mug. The great game in the dinner queue was to hit another person's plate/mug with the corner of your mug to chip off his enamel and get the owner into disciplinary trouble. It was warlike, aggressive... and very unpleasant. The training was tough: feet raw and exhausted with night watch duties from midnight until 4am. The time passed with a blur.

I was transferred to HMS Ceres at Cleckheaton in Yorkshire for three months' training as a victualler. It was a Wrens' camp and the Navy decided that victualling rum and tobacco was akin to my civvy job of weights and measures. The Wrens had a civilising effect on the recruits and the discipline was less authoritarian and the food almost edible. Nevertheless two of our intake of thirty committed suicide and one was dismissed for what I now realise was homosexuality. I had never heard of homosexuality at the time. I played rugby and discovered that, in the Navy, sport opened every door.

I was put under a lot of pressure by the Commander and the Padre to sign on and take a permanent officer commission. I strung them along for a time but never signed the papers as it meant I would be signing away my freedom for five or seven years. The rugby mad Padre couldn't believe I would turn down such a wonderful life opportunity. I vividly remember his disbelieving interview on my last day when he was absolutely scathing about my working-class background and proposed career in weights and measures. "How will you ever amount to anything that could compare with this?"

However, at the end of my initial training I was given a letter of introduction to the Rear Admiral in charge of Devonport Services Rugby Team. A reputation had preceded me and the Western Evening Mail had, quite wrongly, been full of news of a new Rugby League star coming to the West Country. (Me !) 'A Second Lewis Jones' ran one headline. (Lewis had preceded me as a national service victualler and had been the star of Welsh rugby and the Great Britain team.) I was given a reasonable billet and relieved of duty watches and spent most of my national service playing rugby for Devonport Services and tennis for the Navy against the Army, Marines and RAF in the Inter-forces Championship at Wimbledon. I won championships in long jump and triple jumping. I wasn't a world-beater at any of these things – the Navy was short of sportsmen – but a pretty good above-average.

One tennis anecdote. In tennis jargon I was known as a 'retriever'. Very fast, very accurate and masses of concentration. I could return most any shot, no matter how hard, but couldn't hit a volley or drive to save my life. In Round 1 and Round 2 at Forces Wimbledon I beat established attacking players in two very attractive matches. In Round 3 I was allocated to Court 2, the one with the seats and paying spectators. I played a man just like me.

Neither of us could volley but we could return shots until the end of time. We were barracked and criticised and by the time we finished the seats were deserted. "Not a shot in them!" I heard one spectator say. I won 6-4, 6-4 in five hours twenty minutes. It must be some sort of record.

However, rugby was my main activity and the camaraderie was quite exceptional. Great rugby sing-songs. The ranks of Officer/Seaman were ignored and I found I had added status as a national serviceman... something that would not have applied in the Army or the RAF. We played Saturday and Wednesday, travelled throughout the UK and stayed in good hotels with real food, so very different from the horrible, inedible meals in barracks.

Sailors were allocated twenty cigarettes a day. I sold mine for two shillings a packet and this provided me with ample spending money. Our wages in 1954-1956 were 28 shillings a week.

National Service was great for me, offering sport and the opportunity to start to mature outside my home environment. But for many of my contemporaries it seemed an empty experience, treading water for two wasted years. 'Skiving' (avoiding work) was warmly applauded and for sailors there was the daily mind-numbing tot of Pusser's Rum, a tradition which extended back for three hundred years but which was discontinued in 1970. Junior ratings over twenty years of age lined up each day to receive, and instantly consume their 'grog', one eighth of a pint of rum plus two measures of water. The challenge was to arrange some official work at noon and then be entitled to collect the rum informally in the early evening. The neat rum (called 'neaters') could then be saved as the pre-prandial to a weekend binge (a 'snifter' to get everyone 'lubricated' or 'loaded') or used as barter for favours. There was a complex and ingenious system of measurement used in bartering, which appealed to my 'weights and measures' mind. A 'sipper' of rum was offered for small favours, a 'gulper' for money, cigarettes or something more significant, and a 'sandy bottom', the whole tot, for a substantial benefit like deputising cover for a duty watch. These informal arrangements were seen as a significant triumph over 'the system'.

Only a very small proportion of ratings would have been able to outwit the system: out of perhaps a couple of thousand ratings issued with grog at midday, only thirty or forty would manage to get neat rum in the evenings. Of these, some would drink it immediately, having no money to go out, others would use it for barter and a few would save it for a binge, even several days' tots if they could. The 'neaters' would usually be drunk in advance of the binge which took place in port, off ship or barracks. Naval ratings were always inspected and often searched before going ashore. The rum would be confiscated if found – a huge risk never worth taking.

In October 1955 I dislocated my shoulder trying to tackle the great Welsh wing three-quarter Gwyn Jones in a game against Newport - the great power of the day. More dislocations followed and in December I was given the choice of the 'Bancroft' shoulder operation or never playing rugby again. I had been tipped as a possible England player and there was no argument... except from my mother... So the operation it was, and this took me almost through to demobilisation in June 1956. The scar was butchery but it was followed by five very pleasant months of exercise, convalescence and physiotherapy.

On my twentieth birthday, I lined up at midday for my first official daily issue of Navy grog. It was a daunting experience. Long lines of ratings inside Devonport Barracks, HMS Drake. My turn came too quickly. A salute, my number and a half-pint glass into which was ladled the measure of rum and double of water, to drink all-in-one. The grog seared and burned my throat and I felt as though a jet of tears burst from my eyes, completely missing my cheekbones. There was no question of delay or a second swallow as the whole exercise was timed for ten seconds and to take longer would be deemed 'sissy'. I managed to stay upright as I marched out of the great hall but think I remained in a semi-alcoholic stupor until the date of my demobilisation four weeks later.

BACK IN OLDHAM

With accumulated leave I was back in Oldham at the end of June 1956 but couldn't start work at Weights and Measures until 8 August, i.e. exactly two years after I left. I needed money and signed on as a casual worker in the Parkona Bakery Ltd, which had just won a Marks and Spencer catering contract.

It was my first sight of bad management: appalling industrial relations and a work-shy and irresponsible workforce. Each day shift had to produce just two enormous vats of cake mix ready for cooking. The men whispered we had to do things slowly: staff never did anything unless the Foreman was 'on their back' and they would, whenever possible, sabotage the mixture. Chaps were always disappearing to play card games in the WC. The favourite scam was to put a handful of raisins in a batch of angel cake (should be plain) which had taken three hours to prepare. The managers would panic and instead of taking disciplinary action would offer everyone huge bonuses to complete a replacement mix at breakneck speed.

My pay packet was quite healthy and I gave it unopened to my mother. This was the working-class custom of the day. Indeed I continued to give my pay packet to my mother for the next six months and Mother gave me my pocket money in return. She was more generous than my needs and we only negotiated a rent contribution when Aunty Ann pointed out that I wasn't 'learning the value of money'. That got my dad's attention. Two years later I was a rugby professional with money coming out of my ears.

My main preoccupation was a desire to study and pass my Final professional exams. I appreciated that I couldn't again prey on my mother's time as they had just bought the corner shop on Gainsborough Avenue. They both worked very hard and we all discovered there is much more to a shop than simply selling to customers. I went to a special night school class, again at Ducie Avenue, and also studied for three hours immediately after work and on Sunday afternoons. That meant I could continue with a very active social life/rugby training from 8pm every evening. I studied hard and scarcely missed a day of study except Christmas. Prevailing wisdom was that it would take three or four years to qualify. Dan Davies, the grammar school recruit ahead of me, had already failed his Finals on five occasions.

However, I persuaded the Chief Inspector to enter and pay for me to attempt the February 1957 Board of Trade exam in London. Jack Stainthorpe was my ally. He said I would gain valuable experience of the pressure of the exams and the aggressive oral and practical. This might give me a realistic chance of success in 1958. Reluctantly Oldham agreed and, interestingly, it was my future father-in-law Cllr Fred Holden, Chairman of the Council's Watch Committee, who authorised the expenditure.

I passed with distinction, the youngest qualified inspector in the UK, too young to take up appointment as I was below the statutory minimum age of twenty-one years. Dan also passed, on his sixth attempt, after nine years of study. What I didn't know was that behind the scenes the department, still a police department, had a problem: there was only one vacant inspector's post. Dan was very well liked and had worked hard for his qualification. However, the Chief and the Committee had spotted me as a potential high-flier whose services should be retained.

Dan and I were both given a good rise in salary but no appointment. We put this down to bureaucratic inefficiency, without knowing anything of the tug-of-war behind the scenes. In due course two posts were created, quite an unusual local government event in those days. This solved the dilemma and we were both appointed.

The weights and measures exam, the 'Board of Trade Exam', had been conducted by the government for almost a hundred years. Despite a well-qualified intake, the pass rate rarely exceeded twenty per cent with many candidates attempting to pass time and time again. The infamous Mr Corns of Cheshire County Council failed thirty-three attempts despite having given learned legal papers at conferences and seminars. The scope was narrow but the detail very deep, especially the law and engineering papers. Many could shine in one area but would plummet in another. But I was 'Lucky Jim'.

far enough away to get away with" and I was curious to know whether my skills were transferable.

I arrived in Leigh at 10am to find I was not travelling with the A Team but had been selected for the 1st v Dewsbury under the pseudonym 'J Harrison'. The legendary international Jim Ledgard was full-back for Dewsbury. I had a sensational introduction and scored four impressive tries. The match finished and I was whisked into the oak-panelled boardroom and treated like God. They took two hours to get my signature and agree a contract worth £3,000. By comparison, our first three-bedroomed house cost only £1,900. They kept me absolutely incommunicado but then no one, except my dad, knew where I was. However, several of the top clubs – Wigan, Leeds, Salford, St Helens – had sent their spies. All had contacted Dad and Uncle Fred Humble, offering them mind-boggling amounts for my signature. When I eventually returned home on cloud nine, it was too late.

I never regretted my decision. I was well treated at Leigh. We could earn as much as £100 for a winning game but only £7 losing pay. This was at a time when top professional soccer players, e.g. Manchester United, could not earn more than £20 per week. My payments at Easter and Christmas equalled my annual local government weights and measures salary.

I had some memorable games, though only lasted elev minutes after receiving a fractured eye socket against New Zealand team. I scored a number of hat-tricks and he satisfaction of getting the winning tries against

GIRLFRIENDS

I had had occasional girlfriends from time to time, nothing serious, as sport, study and beer were my obsessions. However, I had filled out in the twelve months after demob, having put on two stones. Some of it was muscle! Also my salary had increased from about £180 per annum to £520… I felt rich. I bought a little blue van as commercial vehicles were exempt from Excise Duty. New. £300. I also discovered I was reasonably popular when I staggered into the Froggarts or Hill Stores dance halls at pub closing time. I was a good dancer, having been persuaded by my friend Terry Cooper to take dancing lessons at Billington's Dance Academy.

A couple of girlfriends stand out in my mind. My most serious girlfriend was a teacher, Kathleen Mitchell, the younger sister of Brian, a close rugby friend. Her family liked me and I liked Kathleen; and Aunty Ann certainly approved of her red hair.

We started 'going regular' during my national service or, at least, I enjoyed her regular flow of entertaining letters. We didn't actually see each other very much. When I demobbed we were indulged by Uncle Fred and Aunty Ann Rhodes and went out to dinner with them at least once a week with me driving Fred's rather grand Morris Oxford. Aunty Ann's latent hostility to Freda and the Holdens is probably something to do with having found a kindred spirit in Kathleen. Indeed we might have married although I never recall having actually made a proposal. In 1958 I had applied for and got a job in Kenya at the zenith of the Mau Mau. My mother was terrified but thought it would be all right if I married and went with Kathleen. Kathleen and I agreed but her mother wouldn't let her go, married or not. So that was that! Such innocent compliant days.

My other memory is Barbara Lewis, a stunningly beautiful librarian and a friend of Margaret, my sister. We started dating shortly after I became an affluent rugby professional and she suited the image I thought I deserved. Ugh! I was so juvenile. I was very much the envy of the team and we could easily have auditioned for an old-time Footballers' Wives. Barbara was replaced by Freda and she eventually went to Spain and married a bullfighter. Freda tells a story that she and I met at a party and I must have flirted. Freda was approached by Barbara and told to "Get your hands off my man". At the time getting involved with me was not something Freda had thought of doing. She says! But I knew Freda was 'the one' and it probably showed.

RUGBY

I hope not to write much about rugby. There is a huge t of news cuttings somewhere in my attic. I described first game with Oldham Rugby Union Club when I sixteen years old in the 'Colts Rugby' chapter, and ur 'National Service' I described how while in the Nav played for Devonport Services RFC and various comb services and representative teams. My oft-disloc shoulder thwarted my expected elevation to greater th This culminated in a messy operation and five plec months of recuperation. In the whole of my two years i Royal Navy I never did one single duty watch, never di task of my job of victualling. It was sport, sport, sport Navy gave great support to the few talented na servicemen who came into their clutches.

By the time I returned to Oldham I had missed on season and, during 1957/58, I reoriented myself a Lane. The following season I was thrilled to be el Captain and saw myself as 'over the hill'. I had nc slightest thought or ambition of ever becom professional. We had a stunning season and I had a ha tries when we faced a February freeze-up of sign proportion. I was frustrated to miss two Saturday The following weekend match was called off again and vulnerable to a stout man with cloth cap who whis "Would you like a game with the other code?" I ha refusing rugby league scouts' offers for years and v have dreamed of playing in the Oldham area. Howev offer was an A Team game at Leigh and I thought "

Wigan and Oldham. However, the experience I most enjoyed was the one and only A Team game I ever played. There had been a lot of controversy in Oldham when I signed for Leigh, with fans threatening to sack the Board for missing out on a local 'star' signing. Those hostile said I had a 'glass shoulder'. Oldham and Leigh arranged a special match, right at the end of the 60/61 season, with each side agreeing to field half the 1st Team and half potential stars of the future. I could do nothing wrong. I scored five length of the field tries before about 5,000 spectators including all my old friends at the Oldham Rugby Union Club. It was an amazing crowd for a second-class match.

Mick Martyn and Ray Fisher, Great Britain players with whom I was about to go on a six-week French/Spanish holiday, and the other 1st Team players went on a pub crawl in Oldham. Everybody in every pub seemed to know me or at least know the result of what was officially billed an A Team match. It was an out-of-body experience.

I played on the wing. My strength was 'speed off the mark' and an ability to tackle my opponent before he had time to gather speed. Indeed I saw all matches as a duel between my opposite number and me. Not so today. I succeeded well against the world famous Billy Boston (Wigan) and Brian Bevan (Warrington) but thought Tom Van Vollenhoven (St Helens) the greatest player of all time. Powerful, fast, elusive: it was like trying to contain a monster electric eel.

I could write a lot about rugby but will describe only two further incidents. We had quite a rough and dirty set of forwards. Derek Hurt, second row, could 'walk up' legs in the scrum and contort his body to pulverize an opponent's knees. Horrible. Genial gigantic Stan Owen invariably lost his temper. Against Oldham he thought the loose forward Bryn Day had fouled him. The scrum settled in the middle of the field. Up stood Stan and knocked the Oldham player unconscious. Red card. As he approached the wing he was mobbed by four or five enraged Oldham supporters who were left prostrate. An incautious policeman decided to intervene. Out like a light. I still have the vision of bodies lying all over the pitch as Stan was apprehended and taken to 'the cooler'. He was detained overnight. I was the only Leigh player who lived in Oldham and was sent to bail him out the following day. Stan was still in his rugby gear and he roared with laughter to see me. He was a lovely man.

We always had a tough game at Whitehaven. There was then a beautiful single-line railway which ran along the coast from Carlisle, and you felt you had reached the end of the world. They had a particularly partisan set of spectators and one of the local characters was a large woman in long black coat and broad-brimmed black hat who sat near the in-goal touchline. For some reason she took a dislike to me and berated me for dirty play. In truth I never deliberately fouled an opponent. After one tackle I heard the crowd roar and found her on the pitch chastising me with an umbrella. I made off with an exaggerated run and she chased. I am told it was the funniest thing ever seen on a professional rugby field. Passions were high. After the match, irate Whitehaven fans barricaded us in our dressing room for two hours.

COURTSHIP

I had admired Freda for a long time. My first 'sighting' was walking home from East Oldham High School (later called Counthill Grammar) in 1949/50 across Red Flats, Oldham. I saw a bunch of my fee-paying friends from other schools all chasing a shrieking girl. The friends Reg Langton, Gordon Marr, Ian Simpson, Malcolm Whitney and John Nuttall had an extra day's holiday. I watched the proceedings which the attractive girl seemed to be enjoying. I was curious to see the boys were trying to scratch their nails across the girl's face, neck, legs or arms to raise huge red and white welts. It was astonishing; and Freda, because that's who it was, seemed happy to allow me to scratch the back of her hand and observe the biological transformation. It was a condition known as dermographism. She stuck in my mind.

We later met in 1952 playing tennis in Copster Park when she and her sister Shirley were the leaders of the 'moneyed' slightly upper-middle-class section of Oldham teenage society. I had a couple of dates with Shirley but we were always a foursome with Freda and some other chap. I aspired to go out with Freda but never rated my chances. My family will know that, at our 40th Wedding Anniversary in 2002, I quoted my 'star rating' as it appeared in Freda's ancient diary. This made her furious, a reaction I still don't understand as the diary was over fifty years old. I was only trying to say that being 'starred' in her diary in 1952 must have been part of the 'genes of chance' which later led to a long and happy marriage.

My next sighting was in 1958 when I was working at Weights and Measures and Captain of Oldham Rugby Union. Freda was on teaching practice at Werneth School. Everyone went home for lunch. When going back to work, it was my practice to race the bus up the hilly Copster Hill Road as part of my training. Freda got off the bus and I was dazzled. I clearly remember the full, broad-striped, multi-coloured skirt or blue and white, candy-striped dress she invariably wore. Over a period of two or three months, the regular passengers and conductor observed my running. They cheered me on. Freda never noticed - said she never noticed - though we smiled from time to time. I decided there and then that she was the person I would marry. I remember confiding in Jack Stainthorpe and he said, "Good catch. Her father is Chairman of the Council's Watch Committee. You will be marrying the boss's daughter."

The next time I saw her was 1960 at a party at Tony Elgin's father's house. He was the owner of the Ford franchise in South-East Lancashire. At this time I was a well-known local sportsman. I had gone to the party with the beautiful Barbara Lewis. Freda was there, I don't know with whom, but all the memories of my desires came flooding back. I tried to chat her up and Barbara must have noticed my waning attention – even if Freda didn't. That would explain the 'keep your hands off my boyfriend' aggression which I mentioned earlier.

I discovered she was working at Hollinwood Secondary School having recently been ill teaching in Nottingham. She agreed to a date and we saw the premier of the musical play

'Stop the World I Want to Get Off'. It had just opened at a theatre in Manchester.

She was bright, enthusiastic and chatty and knew much, about books, art and the theatre. I was aware she compensated for my cultural deficiencies. I also knew she was special and I wanted to marry her. Not necessarily then, but later. I was determined and dedicated in my pursuit. I had the confidence, or arrogance, of knowing many Oldham mothers viewed me as a good catch. I was never put out when she tried to finish with me. I knew we were right for each other and she had just got a bit muddled. I was right. Of course!

WEDDING

We became engaged in the summer of 1961 when I formally sought permission from her father Alderman and Mayor George Frederick Holden. It was a bit like a Victorian melodrama and he told me what a worry she had been to him because of her diabetes. He was pleased to have had a marriage proposal and thought I was getting an 'attractive and perky' wife. We had a glass of port. He was very proud of being Tory Leader of Oldham in what, sixty years before, had been Winston Churchill's first parliamentary seat.

Her mother Nancy Holden took charge of all the arrangements: the venue Werneth Park Conservatory, the invitations, the church, and a whole raft of speakers who were due to perform with the help of verses composed by Aunty Nene. (We have a compact disc of the whole ceremony.) My best man Jack Stainthorpe was told what he could and could not say, i.e. no innuendo, no ruderies. It was a brilliant wedding, which my family loved.

I married Freda at St Margaret's Church, Oldham on 28 April 1962. It was the last match of the season against Leeds. I had had special dispensation to 'rest'. However, the whole of the Leigh rugby team stopped off in Oldham and enlivened the evening's festivities. Aunty Jenny Ainsworth said it was the very best evening of her life as the compère organised Musical Ladies time and time again. There was one fewer lady on the dance floor each time and when the music stopped a man had to carry a woman to a chair. She loved being grabbed by a massively strong rugby forward and hoisted shoulder high. My male relations and work colleagues were no match for the Leigh players. Memories have it, that cousin Neil Ainsworth launched himself, to save his mother, into an all-out flying tackle on Ted Brophy, our South African star. Ted never noticed and Neil bounced a good ten yards across the dance floor. By then we were long gone on our honeymoon.

Our one regret was that we never obtained photos. It seems the proofs were given to younger brother Robin Holden and he handed them out rather than taking orders. Robin, an amazing character, was also in trouble for raiding his father's wine and spirit stocks and distributing extra alcohol to all and sundry. We spent our honeymoon at the Shakespeare Hotel, Stratford and when we came home I had the offer of a job in Nigeria.

The summer went in a rush as there was so much preparation for the forthcoming trip to Africa. My only clear memory is eating meals of roast chicken with plastic insides. Neither Freda nor I realised that the giblets in the carcass were in plastic bags. We sailed from Liverpool in September 1962, seen off by our fathers Joe Humble and Fred Holden.

NIGERIA

I was interviewed to be the Nigerian Deputy Superintendent of Weights and Measures in October 1960. This was several months before I proposed marriage to Freda. After the interview I went to Soho with another candidate and had my first Chinese meal, a wonderful dish of 'sweet and sour pork': astonishing. It was unlike anything I had ever tasted. I heard nothing back from the interview until nineteen months later. A letter offering me the job was on the mat when we returned from our honeymoon in Stratford-upon-Avon in May 1962.

In the interim I had proposed to Freda, bought and decorated a house at 2 Link Lane, Oldham and got married. Despite having to leave our new house and our families, Freda was firmly in favour. I accepted, much to the distress of my mother and grandmother. They had already begun to anticipate babies. However, we stalled until September and sailed aboard HMS Apapa on the Denver Line. The journey by sea took just over three weeks and Freda became acutely embarrassed because I claimed all the prizes aboard ship. I was super-fit and over-competitive.

Nigeria was a revelation: a wonderful four-year experience which gave me enormous confidence in management at an early age. I lectured, arranged tours to every part of the country with teams of student inspectors, managed budgets, purchased supplies, issued press releases and helped draft legislation and prepare speeches for Federal ministers alongside my boss Laurie Theobald and colleague Ian Welch. The students were good fun, hard-working and academically brilliant – very different from the condemnatory characterisations which then appeared in the British press. Several remain in touch and Swithin Toby and his daughter stayed with us this year. We were delighted to learn he had been knighted Sir Swithin after retiring as Chief Executive Rivers State. I surmise it was because he acted as intermediary between the international oil companies and the polluted villagers – a hot political issue.

Nigeria has a climate of extremes from the arid, skin-cracking, dust-laden, laterite roads of the North to the sweaty, humid, mosquito-riddled, jungle vegetation of the South – where it was sometimes desirable to change clothes several times a day. In 1963 my mother-in-law Nancy Holden circulated extracts from the initial letters we sent home. These offer a more detailed picture of our life at that time and are reproduced, in full, in Appendix B.

I will describe here one unique experience. Freda had been recruited to teach English to the Emir's fourth wife – a giggling fourteen-year-old girl. I was invited to visit the harem whilst the Emir was on tour. Narrow corridors in the Palace led to a huge dark bedroom dominated by a vast ten-square-metre bed with masses of cushions. The walls were adorned with floor to ceiling shelves of brass plate and the only item of furniture was the most enormous American jukebox I had ever seen. Some twenty or more ancient-looking women crowded behind to catch their first glimpse of a white male. It was a far cry from the Hollywood versions. They seemed to want to touch my arm to check the skin was real. We went home wiser and with two live ducks as gifts.

Gifts, bribes or 'dash' were a major blight on the country. My students, colleagues and all the officials I met were appalled and condemnatory about corruption. I had some direct experiences: a chief constable taking bribes from traders in a cotton market just after he had been released from prison for fraud; my steward Garaba having to pay bribes to obtain routine job application forms and even to have his urine tested; departmental papers showing a local emir claimed mileage on the basis that his sixty government-issue cars had been on non-stop travel at 60mph for 365 days of the year; and uncontested headlines stating the Minister of Defence stole the whole cost of one of seven fighter planes purchased from the West German Government. Friends told more lurid stories. Most traced the seed of corruption to the original activities of the United Africa Company, anxious to bribe locals to repel commercial competition.

Nigeria was also the scene of my proudest personal moment, walking on air, bursting and strutting with pleasure and pride. The place: Kingsway store in Kano, the month: June 1964, and on my hip baby Josephine, five months old... the most beautiful and perfect creature I had ever seen. It was the beginning of our second tour and Freda and Joey had flown from England six weeks later than I. Freda needed rest but Joey was ready to be taken out shopping by Daddy after the weeks of separation. I wanted the whole world to see my baby daughter and knew no one would ever take the smile off my face. They haven't. Sadly, this was the month that Grampy, Freda's father, died, as well as my grandmother Tamar Rhodes. We were in Nigeria with water strikes and long postal delays. The funerals were long past before we got any information.

The last year in Nigeria - 1965 - was the most difficult year. Trouble was in the air. The regional governments were targeting Federal employees. I had fourteen staff arrested in Eastern Region on some trumped-up dishonesty charges. It was alleged that the official fees collected and in their possession were bribes. I attended court and was able to show that all monies in their possession were fees and had been properly entered into the government account books. They were released with much rejoicing.

My return to Lagos coincided with the conclusion of the Federal Government's treason trial against the charismatic Leader of the Opposition Chief Obafemi Awolowo. His Yoruba supporters flooded the streets. The world press arrived and trouble was in the air. All non-essential Federal employees, including me, were given 'gardening leave'. But after three days we went back to work, adjacent to the Central Court. The crowds were in very good-natured high spirits: High-Life music and dance. There was no trouble at all. The press seemed disappointed and I met a number of bored journalists and photographers who boasted about paying Yoruba supporters to throw smoke bombs and stage mock battles for the benefit of pictures in UK tabloid newspapers. I subsequently developed a fairly healthy scepticism for parts of the tabloid press.

We were burgled one night in Lagos and everything was stolen from downstairs, including crockery, carpets, easy chairs, and the key to the French windows. Because of the missing key I made a great fuss about security and we were allocated a policeman. At 3am the next night there was another commotion. I looked out of the bedroom window and saw the policeman running in one direction and a group of ten or twelve 'tiefmen' running in another. The 'tiefmen' had used the stolen keys but had been disturbed already climbing the stairs to our bedroom. For the first time we hired a permanent 'myguardie' armed with a four-foot machete.

In summer 1965 the Western Yoruba problem seemed to have receded but the skirmishes between the Northern Hausa and the Eastern Egbos, which became the Biafran War, had already started. I should make it clear that throughout the whole of my contract I was treated with considerable support and respect, most particularly by Muslims. I had no hesitation about continuing my travels if we came to embryonic battle lines. I reported to the local military commander and asked if the shooting could be stopped whilst we travelled through. I was ushered onwards with absolute courtesy and felt completely safe and secure. Six months after I left, the position changed. Europeans were threatened and some had distressing experiences. At Kano Airport some of my friends trying to leave the country were separated from sixty or seventy Ebo (Egbo) Nigerians. The Egbos were slaughtered in front of them. We have become familiar with horrendous events today. In 1966 they were unbelievable.

Worst for the family, in Freda's final week our precious baby Josephine got a Tumba fly. We had known about Tumba flies for four years but never seen one. They lay eggs on clothes; the eggs hatch into grubs which burrow through pores into the human body where they grow and grow. Freda, heavily pregnant with Becca, discovered baby Josephine had a large red lump on her thigh. We smeared the top of the lump with Vaseline to block any air hole. Out crawled a wriggling white grub. Horrible.

Overall I wouldn't have missed Nigeria for the world. I continue to view the country and its people with great affection. The Nigerians I met were lovely, bright, hard-working, intelligent, hospitable and considerate people. Freda and I had lots of adventures and made lifelong friends (such as Lyn Strover, Chris Gant and Sue Brookes). I gained great professional experience and inner confidence. I finished my tour in late autumn 1965, having secured job interviews in over thirty local authorities. Trading standards officers were in big demand. I had three months' leave. Becca was born.

HOLIDAYS

I have already mentioned a traumatic holiday incident when I was seven years old. Indeed, all my juvenile holidays were taken on the Lancashire Coast, at Bispham in Blackpool or on the vast golden sands of Southport during Oldham Wakes Week, which later became a whole fortnight. It was an agreed date towards the end of June when all the Oldham cotton mills and businesses closed down. I adored Blackpool – the piers, the penny-slots, the Tower and the Pleasure Beach. Visits today still give a tingle.

I didn't go abroad until I was twenty-one, when I travelled with Neil, Roy and Betty Ainsworth to a campsite in Juan-les-Pins on the French Riviera. Travel by car took a whole week each way and there was strict exchange control over pounds sterling. The maximum amount of money, per person, that could be taken out of the UK was £10. We couldn't speak French so imagine our shock on day one when we purchased a loaf of bread costing the equivalent of 50p. We almost went home. It took some time to discover we had purchased a rather expensive cake.

I went again three years later with professional rugby friends Mick Martyn and Ray Fisher. Loaded with money, we took the French Riviera by storm. We stayed at the famous Hotel Negresco in Nice and won – and lost – at Monte Carlo. After six weeks in the sunshine I returned to have tea with Freda and she claims it was the time I 'turned her head' by looking like a bronzed Adonis. Her words not mine.

We had a wonderful series of holidays with the children until they eventually peeled off to university. Early years were spent camping in France or Italy and later, when we were joined by the Boltons and their lovely children Ben, Charlotte and Emma, we upgraded to a series of apartments or *gîtes*. Travelling to and from our destinations was always enjoyable as we took potluck in staying overnight in small family hotels. Great food and memorable incidents.

We continued to holiday every year with Ann and Eric (now Professor) Bolton and have managed to visit almost every tourist destination in the world: America (East, West and the Oregon Trail), India, South Africa, Kenya, Australia, Hong Kong, China, Russia, Malaysia, Indonesia, Peru, Brazil, Argentina, Mexico, Vietnam and East and West Europe. We shared our 25th Wedding Anniversary – indeed every anniversary - with Gordon and Jeannie Lees (married same year, same day, same time as us) and with Gerry and Janet Dodd on a fantastic Nile Cruise. I have never been so gobsmacked. Everyone should strive for that experience.

Since retirement we continue to go abroad but the best holidays now, the very best holidays, are those we are able to share with our grandchildren. The current deal is that we are willing to go anywhere anytime with any of them, if the parents think we can give support or do a bit of babysitting. We hope that we have not… yet… become a drag or a bore. We try to remain alert. Who knows?

DAUGHTERS

Our first daughter Josephine was born on 4 January 1964. I have already said she was the most beautiful thing I had ever seen. I was working in Kano and had expected to arrive home before the birth in February. However, immediately after Christmas 1963, Nanny Holden placed a call from Oldham to Kano. Telephone connections took three days. She said I should "Come home immediately" as our first-born was due to be induced. I actually arrived in London on 5 January and rang from Heathrow in blinding rain. The ward nurse said I had a daughter and all was well. I hopped a flight to Manchester, a taxi to a florist in Oldham and onwards to Boundary Park Hospital. Freda was absolutely glowing, and sweet Josephine was in the room. She always slept on her tummy and at a very early age she could push her head off the mattress like a tortoise. Funny and unusual. My parents were 'over the moon'.

They were equally delighted when, at the age of seven years, she won the Blue Peter prize for her limerick
There once was a cat called Pat,
Who grew most incredibly fat,
She sat on the floor
And ate more and more,
And that was the end of that.

Rebecca was born on 21 September 1965 just after I returned from our second tour of Nigeria. I was attending interviews for a job in the UK. I had options of thirty interviews and it was really a question of where we wanted to live. On 20 September I had been offered jobs in

Leicestershire and Southend and was staying the night in St Albans with Ian and Pauline Welch prior to an 11am interview at Bury St Edmunds, Suffolk. We rang the hospital at 8.30am to be told 'no change'. I was interviewed by a committee of councillors and the Chairman said, "If we appoint you, we don't want to have any of your slick London tricks." I was appalled because I was from Lancashire, not London. Immediately after the interview I rang the hospital again to be told I had had a daughter at 7am. I left the other candidates and drove hotfoot to Oldham arriving at about 5 o'clock. Saw teeny tiny Becca with a mass of bottles and tubes. Early next morning I left for interviews in London. The Croydon Chief, Cliff Wilson, said, "I don't like Southerners. You're from the North: you can have the job." No questions. We were an unemployed family of four. I took the job and never regretted the decision.

Sarah was born in Croydon on 29 October 1966 and I was determined to witness the birth. Well! Freda was very determined on my behalf. Explicit permission was obtained from the GP, the Consultant and the Houseman. It amounted to nothing. When the time came the nurse in charge ejected me from the room and I spent the whole of the birthing period arguing with the nurses, a venetian blind and a closed door. Then someone said "It's a girl" and although I had anticipated a boy, I was instantly thrilled. It was the perfect family.

They were lovely girls, blond, pretty, close in age and drew ripples of attention almost everywhere we went. Josephine, the eldest, was the leader and the two 'little ones' invariably vied for her attention. Josephine was always conscientious and adored animals: rabbits, hamsters, gerbils, lambs, goat and cat. She had great patience. We thought it likely she would eventually seek a career in Africa or India studying nature 'red in tooth and claw'.

Rebecca was the organised daughter: neat, tidy and methodical. She knew where everything was and did her homework on time. She liked girlie things from a very early age and when I produced a 'boy's' racing car as a surprise present she wept with disappointment. The whole of the family came to rely on Becca for shopping needs and household management. She determined to become a nurse or work in a hospital from the age of six or seven years. Her view never changed and it makes us happy that she remains so fulfilled with her work in Physiotherapy.

Sarah was our lateral thinker. It would be fair to say she was not the tidiest or most organised person in the world. But she had amazing insights about life or art and circumstance. Her homework was usually completed between cereals and toast at breakfast time but invariably got excellent marks. As a small child she sang long creative stories which entertained everyone. And she was competitive, very competitive, perhaps like her father. She probably has the 'Ward' genes.

When the girls were 10, 11 and 12 years old we had a rejected kid goat brought by Nanny Holden from Oldham, a delightful creature called Bilbo. It ate every plant and flower in the garden but never a blade of grass. I was a member of Croham Hurst Golf Club and the three girls took the goat across the road to the fringe of the course to munch weeds and thistles. The club captain objected and I received an official written warning. Two months later, at a charity day, the girls paid an entry to the course to collect autographs. They took the goat on a silver chain. The club captain was livid and threatened my expulsion. I was saved only because the rules forbade cattle and dogs only – goats are neither. It remains a *cause célèbre* at Croham Hurst.

What I did not initially realise is that my marriage to Freda came with another bonus... two actually. First, her mother Nancy Holden who was absolutely wonderful to me and the girls. She had amazing energy, bubbled with ideas and unfailingly encouraged and supported everyone in the family. Every visit she made to Croydon was an absolute delight. The second bonus was Nancy's elder sister Aunty Nene (Irene Boyd) who spent almost all her life, rigid, in a wheelchair but with the most magnificent brain. She was a keen debater and had vast linguistic, literary and cultural knowledge. She prompted and trained my thinking in a myriad of subtle ways. Hers was an extraordinary life and she was, quite simply, the most inspiring person I have ever known. (See 'Irene Remembers' - Cockasnook Books.)

However, this record is not really about my daughters or other members of the family. There are other records. It is about my perceptions of incidents in my life. I will just say I loved every one of them. My daughters all have lovely personalities; they have achieved much and made me so proud. They still do.

CROYDON

Trading Standards Croydon. I was pleased with the job in Croydon. The office was smart and new and the Chief, EC Wilson, was a supporter. London was also a good location to welcome the many expatriate friends we had made in Nigeria. Within six months I was appointed Deputy Chief and observed Chief Wilson to be one of the greater shirkers in local government. From the time of my appointment in 1966 to his discharge in 1971 he did little work. He altered or invented inspection statistics, arrived late morning, dozed or drank, and left for home by 3pm.

It was scandalous but I loved it. I was the youngest *de facto* Chief Inspector in the country and I could experiment with new enforcement techniques without final responsibility. I had long considered routine 'once a year' inspection of every retail premise to be a waste. I changed our priorities to focus on sharp practice and fraud leaving the majority of honest traders free from bureaucracy. I quadrupled verification income by helping to design a multi-tester on non-drip measures. The main manufacturer was based in Croydon. I also tried to write interesting or provocative papers for the Croydon Committee and developed good relationships with local and national journalists, most notably Paul Williams, Telegraph Group.

In 1968 I was the country's leading expert on the Trade Descriptions Act and spokesman for my profession. With WHICH Magazine we opened the first ever Consumer Advice shop in Croydon. I appeared on a regular Jimmy Young TV show speaking about better consumer protection.

In 1971 I was appointed Chief Inspector, given Chief Officer status and found myself the second highest paid chief in the country.

All ex-Rugby League players were banned from playing Rugby Union, for life. However, no one noticed when I captained the Nigerian team against Ghana in Accra and Croydon was a long way from the hotbeds of League, 'the real man's game'. I therefore slunk quietly to play for Warlingham RUFC, Surrey. I told no one about my background. No one. It was a fun time – tremendous kindness, hospitality and good spirits – and as an 'old head' I played in the centre alongside Terry Brooke, later Harlequins and England. We did well, but unfortunately I was unable to avoid being selected for a match between London Counties and Middlesex.

The following week the magazine Rugby World included in its jottings "Was the Jim Humble who played against Middlesex the same Humble who played Northern League?" I resigned from Warlingham immediately and was not allowed to set foot in a Rugby Union ground until 1997 when Rugby Union itself became professional.

Our social life in Croydon was great. It centred on Round Table, a wonderful organisation of clubs for young men under the age of forty years. Tablers who moved from one location to another had instant access to a welcoming group of like-minded friends. Monthly dinner meetings attracted good speakers and each year a different set of members was elected to devise innovative charitable events, debates and rip-roaring social functions. As Chairman of Addiscombe and Shirley Table in 1970 I was seconded to help organise the National Conference at Alexandra Palace. The last night fancy dress ball was sensational with over 5,000 revellers. Kenny Ball performed at one end of the dance floor with Acker Bilk at the other. Monty Sunshine was in reserve. We gained enormous self confidence and organisational skills and it is a great pity Round Table is in free-fall decline.

Round Table was exclusive to men and their families. Modern equivalents involve men and women in a more enlightened, even-handed manner. However, it is worth noting that Freda and twelve other wives have continued to meet every month for the past thirty years. The walls have bounced and resonated with their animated discussions about sex, clothes, pregnancy, children, husbands, schools, careers, weddings, separation, divorce, grandchildren, sickness and now... death. The whole gamut of human experience.

OFFICE OF FAIR TRADING

In 1972 there was great political interest in the Government's decision to create an Office of Fair Trading which gave massive new impetus to consumer protection. I thought I would 'throw my hat into the ring' and had a good interview with the Civil Service Commission. I accepted the post of Deputy Director Consumer Affairs and again doubled my salary. On my first day there were fewer than ten people in the Office, which later grew to over six hundred. It was challenging and exciting. In 1973 all government-sponsored information was written formally on white paper. Alongside Dorothy Drake, ex-Punch Editor, we introduced colour, later pictures and even cartoons. I made many TV appearances and had a two-year weekly contract with You and Yours Radio 4.

A principal responsibility was to get written public undertakings from persistent offenders: companies, traders and directors who exploited consumers. Our hit list included used-car dealers, double-glazing salesmen, cowboy builders and the manufacturers of shoddy clothes and footwear. The system, designed to improve behaviour, was slow and ponderous though it could eventually lead to swingeing penalties for contempt of court. However, the more effective sanction was adverse publicity in the local press.

A novel task was to persuade trade associations to launch Codes of Good Practice which gave positive consumer benefits. My initial targets included the travel industry, car manufacturers, and the manufacturers of footwear and domestic appliances. With each code we negotiated four areas of priority: the first to forbid bad practices, the second to provide good consumer information, the third to create a simple complaints procedure and the fourth to set aspirational quality standards. Each code massively improved consumer protection, but they were viewed with some cynicism by regulators and the consumer press. The problem was the absence of an overt punishment when a trader failed to honour a provision in a code. On the other hand, these failures put the leaders of an industry in 'last chance saloon' and the government was able to introduce appropriate legislation with the minimum of opposition. In fact great improvements were made, including truthful labelling, the prohibition of 'small print' contracts and a vastly improved user-friendly system of small claims in the county courts.

That jogs an embarrassing memory. In 1974, the Minister of Trade Sir Geoffrey Howe, the Director-General of Fair Trading and I embarked on a Scottish tour. Our aim was to promote consumer rights and draw attention to the then virtually unknown facility of resolving consumer claims in the county court. In Edinburgh we launched a massive poster campaign: "SCOTLAND – COUNTY COURTS ARE HERE TO HELP YOU". When the applause died down an impassioned Citizens' Advice Bureau worker condemned our metropolitan stupidity: "County courts," he said, "don't exist in Scotland. We have a different system of 'Sheriff Courts'." There was an embarrassed hush. The Minister glared at the Director-General, the Director-General glared at me, and I looked for a hole in the floor. The campaign literature was destroyed and we returned to London with our tails most firmly between our legs. That young Citizens' Advice Bureau worker was a brilliant advocate. Shortly afterwards he was elected to Westminster and died in 2000 the much-loved Leader of the Scottish Parliament, Donald Dewar MP.

My inspiration was Sir John Methven, Director-General. He allowed my ambition and enthusiasm full reign. I was upset when he moved to become Director-General of the CBI and shattered when he died a few months later from a blood clot after a very minor knee operation. He was replaced by Sir Gordon Borrie, a professor of law with whom I had collaborated for many years. His management style was the direct opposite of Sir John's. Methven was extroverted and made policy with a wide sweep whilst Borrie would construct policy piece by piece. I watched and learned and consciously adopted something of both approaches to management.

I had high ratings for the 'Assistant Secretary' grade in the Civil Service and 'the system' wanted me to do well. That meant widening my experience in other departments. However, that was difficult. I was too senior and had not had experience of drafting major legislation or working in a minister's private office at junior level.

The Office of Fair Trading was trying to force change in the Government's attitude to consumers. This led to many inter-departmental committees and meetings. I was steeped in my subject but became enormously impressed by the manner in which senior civil servants were able to 'instantly' analyse and contribute to complicated issues. I particularly enjoyed my work on the Methven Committee [Cmnd 6628] to review trade description laws and a Cabinet Committee on a certain quasi-religious cult – a really quite distasteful organisation. These committees are meetings of top officials representing ministers and are convened in bomb-proof rooms deep below the Treasury. We had many inter-departmental disagreements and a memorable dispute with the Treasury about our splendidly innovative package of consumer materials for secondary schools under the title 'Susie the Supershopper'. The Treasury objected and argued we had exceeded our brief by producing consumer 'education' when we should have limited it to consumer 'information' only. The Director-General as 'accounting officer' would be surcharged. He wasn't, but that early initiative had to be withdrawn.

The job gave me my first opportunity to understand the politics of Europe: Friday mornings in a tiny executive jet to meetings of the Council of Europe in Strasbourg. I chaired a number of working groups of consumer protection officials and, contrary to media speculation, the practical and pragmatic UK approach to regulation invariably won the day.

I was very sad to leave the OFT; it was such a vibrant and innovative organisation. But in 1979 I was chosen to lead a team of top civil servants to the Netherlands and was promoted to an Under-Secretary post as Director of the Metrication Board.

HAGUE 9

The Prime Minister and the premiers of France and the Netherlands agreed that each year they would entertain thirty top civil servants from the other countries to show them every aspect of their politics, life and culture. I felt fortunate to be selected for Hague 9 (ninth year) and even more surprised to be chosen as leader. In essence it meant that I got people out of bed and made about two hundred thank-you speeches. These followed visits to government departments, trade unions, media moguls, commerce and business and all manner of policy and pressure groups. It was a wonderful three months but also the source of my greatest embarrassment.

The day's visit was to the local authority of Gouda. We were late and did not have time for a look around the town before the start of the civic lunch. I was due to make the usual leader's thank-you speech. The Mayor proposed our toast and handed me a beautifully wrapped parcel about the size of a large ovoid tennis ball. I glimpsed its creamy insides and had what I thought was a wonderful bit of repartee: Gouda equals Cheese.

I had already collected no end of flags and medallions so I constructed my peroration to say how 'wonderful' the local authority had been in 'devising a gift which all thirty visitors could eat and share'. There was an audible gasp and a deafening silence. I looked at my zipper. I wondered whether a waiter had collapsed and died. I knew I had done something wrong but didn't know what. I sat down in virtual silence. I opened the parcel and found it contained, not cheese, but a fine, famous, fat candle. Had we looked around the town we would have known that candles rather than cheese are the benchmark of the Gouda community.

METRICATION BOARD

I joined the Board in 1979 under Roy Hattersley, Secretary of State for Trade, and Jim Callaghan, Prime Minister. Margaret Thatcher was Leader of the Opposition and Sally Oppenheim an anti-metric thorn in the sides of my predecessors. I was to mastermind the final thrust to the metric system. The plans and legislation had been made and just needed a signature from the Minister Roy Hattersley. We met. He was enthusiastic but said a general election was about to be announced. He would delay signing until after Labour had won, as any metric initiative might lose votes. Labour lost the election and Thatcher won.

The Board were not dismayed. The Tories had originally pushed for metric and Thatcher was a scientist... Surely she could see advantage. We met. She listened to our brief with hooded eyes and revealed not a flicker of her thinking. Days later she announced the Board was to be abolished.

There was however to be a grand debate in the Lords led by our distinguished past chairman Lord Richie-Calder. Members of the Board, past and present, understandably wanted to be reminded of the decisions they had taken and we stood ready to oblige. Everything was in the public domain. However, officials at the Department of Trade went into a tailspin. I was forbidden to speak to any member of the Board eligible to speak in debate and threatened by official secrets legislation. Perhaps I responded unwisely because the security guards at Millbank Tower were then instructed to prevent the access of Board members. For a short period of time it was quite a dramatic 'storm in a teacup'.

I very much enjoyed the experience of the Board which was different from anything I had previously experienced. Interviews with journalists and radio were invariably hostile. At OFT I had been briefed by sources such as the BBC about the vulnerability of that day's villain. At the Board, I was the villain. Quite a shock. I note that I am still being abused on anti-metric websites some twenty-five years later. I also had to try to find jobs for over fifty staff in other government departments. There were lots and lots of tearful farewell parties and I got to know a great deal about the inner workings of the civil service establishment. In my opinion the cost of metric dithering has cost the country millions of pounds.

I had a memorable experience in Northern Ireland. After I had undertaken metric conferences and radio interviews my hosts arranged a tour of the Province. There were powerful images: a brooding menace on the Shankhill and Falls roads, armour-protected post offices, floral tributes to death on country lanes, and a barbed wire stockade dominating the beautiful village of Crossmaglen. We stopped outside an infants' school at home-time. Our car was surrounded by a class of five-year-olds. They sang to the tune of 'Ring a Ring a Roses' but the words were about 'Killing a British Soldier'. Horrible imagery from the young.

Four hours later our car was detained by the army while queuing at Belfast Airport. My hosts and I were separately interviewed by army officers. "What have you been doing?"

"Where have you been?" "Where did you stay?" I felt very guilty. My mind went blank. I could think only of the army instruction 'Just give name and number'. The awkwardness was soon over but I thought of the many times I had been the confident interrogator and made broad assumptions on the basis of the silence or evasiveness of my interviewee.

I saw out the last days of the Metrication Board like the captain of a sinking ship.

NATIONAL METROLOGICAL COORDINATING UNIT

In my grand suite of offices at the top of Millbank Tower, next to the Tate Gallery, I was beginning to wonder about my next job. I was unfazed. Redundancies were unknown and I was confident a good job would be found. In 1980 it was: I received an offer to be Director of the National Metrological Coordinating Unit, a new governmental agency designed to oversee the introduction of a new 'average' system of weight and measures and to co-ordinate all local authority inspectors. The Civil Service would pay my salary and appoint my board, but local government would find offices and staff and put forward senior councillors for nomination.

The system worked like a dream and representatives of the 400 plus local authorities in England, Scotland, Wales and Northern Ireland thought that the principles being developed within NMCU might have wider application. Enforcement authorities always considered themselves to be 'rugged individualists', confident and able to take decisions which conflicted with the opinions of colleagues. However, this created mayhem for multiples, food manufacturers and tour operators. Advertising and marketing initiatives might be approved by one authority, be modified by a second, and result in prosecution by a third, or fourth or fifth. We therefore developed a system of expert advisory panels and an arrangement which gave a single authority, in the area of a company head office, over-riding jurisdiction. This became known as the 'Home Authority System' and its enthusiastic development was probably my most original contribution to posterity.

LACOTS

In 1982 the Local Authority Associations invited me to resign from the Civil Service. In addition to being Director of the NMCU they wanted me to become Chief Executive of a failing co-ordinating body called LACOTS (now LACORS), Local Authority Co-ordinating Body on Food and Trading Standards. I was to do both jobs. They were jobs which precisely suited my skills and previous experience. I am a conciliator or facilitator by nature and I loved being in the middle of warring groups trying to find consensus.

I was responsible for trading standards, consumer protection, environmental health, public analysts, safety experts, animal inspectors and heavy lorries. I developed the ideas from the NMCU into LACOTS as a whole. The Panel System had over 140 Chief Officer Advisers, Enforcement Guidance Notes and the newly acknowledged, and quite brilliant, Home Authority System - a concept which has since been formalised by legislation and expanded into other services and in other countries.

The job really suited me. It was to change prevailing attitudes amongst potentially hostile audiences, to persuade business to adopt higher voluntary standards and accept enforcement, to persuade enforcers to be consistent and apply common sense rather than the 'letter of the law', to persuade politicians to provide a reasonable adequacy of resources, and to advise consumers to inform and protect themselves, as well as to keep the press 'on side'. It was great, I loved it.

The intensity of support given by local authorities and volunteer chief officers was quite magnificent. Instead of being directed or 'told what to do' by government, local authorities could share best practice and discipline themselves in a practical and effective manner. A novel experience. The key players were called Panel Chairmen and each took responsibility for an area of specialism: food, metrology, product safety or trade descriptions. Many deserve to be mentioned but I would pick out Bryan Beckett (Avon), Noel Hunter (Warwickshire), Paul Allen (East Sussex), Bob Wright (Barnsley), Chris Howell (Dudley), David Sibbert (Oxfordshire CC) and Mike Drewry (Edinburgh) as exceptional.

I guess I also enjoyed the personal publicity and delighted in the range and variety of tasks: from mad cows to timeshare, counterfeit videos to banking fraud, child safety to food labelling, advertising and overloaded lorries to metrology. There were opportunities to travel the world. I was guest speaker at conferences from Oregon USA to Melbourne Australia. I organised a trade conference in Yugoslavia on the day the Berlin Wall came down and appeared on Yugoslav 'Any Questions' TV before being hustled off for a private audience with the Prime Minister.

A particular achievement was the creation of various European co-ordinating agencies, particularly FLEP (the Forum of Food Law Enforcement Practitioners), PROSAFE (Product Safety) and WELMEC (Western European Legal Metrology Cooperative). These organisations are still going strong. WELMEC has long since been extended to Central and Eastern Europe but has nevertheless retained the

'Western' designation. Freda and I continue to enjoy the company of the six who first organised and ran FLEP. I am not sure these would have developed in quite the same manner without my constant prodding. No one seemed to have quite my enthusiasm or wide range of contacts. And I was supported by an absolutely super staff, of whom Ron Gainsford and Lynne Skelton remain most special friends.

I also enjoyed public debates with Tory ministers and with Chris Booker of the Sunday Telegraph and the Daily Mail who relentlessly attacked the alleged overzealousness and inconsistency of environmental health and trading standards officers. The allegations against trading standards were mostly false and I published a booklet demonstrating the mistruths and exaggerations of ministers and the press. LACOTS became a pseudo folk hero in some quarters of local government. However it was not all adulation. Some councillors thought that my agreement to meet ministers prior to the abolition of the metropolitan counties was treacherous. They made quite serious threats; fortunately none were ever implemented.

Local councillors are often characterised as irresponsible, opportunist chancers. In my experience nothing could be further from the truth. In the whole of my time with LACOTS, I found the vast number of councillors to be fair-minded, sensible and with a very strong sense of community commitment. Party politics rarely played a role at national level. It was therefore a surprise and a shock when my Board polarised politically over the measurement of alcohol. One party wanted 'wine by the glass' to be sold by measure whilst the other party insisted only that froth should be excluded from the measurement of a pint of beer. At the time the arguments were heated and lacked compromise. It was very untypical.

In the Queen's birthday honours list in 1993 I was awarded the OBE for services to local government, trading standards and consumer affairs. I know Lynne Skelton secretly did the canvassing. We have a video of the ceremony of pomp and circumstance. I became surprisingly tense at the last moment and I almost 'nutted' the Queen as we came nose to nose. In our brief chat she said I had had quite the longest introduction of the day. That gave me an opening to talk about salmonella, mad cows and counterfeiting. It seemed to arouse a flicker of interest. Only two unmarried daughters were allowed in the Palace so Josephine had to join us at Buckingham Palace gates for our special lunch.

I had the opportunity to meet many interesting people. But I particularly enjoyed parties organised by my LACOTS colleague Lynne Skelton and her flatmate for people from the art world. One charming and articulate guest was an African working with the ANC (African National Congress). He and I were least knowledgeable about 'art' and usually found a quiet corner to exchange experiences of Nigeria, apartheid, corruption, wars and tribal politics. He regularly quizzed me about the prejudices of the 'old' colonials compared with my experiences. That modest man turned out to be Thabo Mbeki, now president of South Africa. He replaced Nelson Mandela, my hero of the twentieth century. Wow!

RETIREMENT

I retired on 1 June 1998, having worked for forty-six immensely satisfying and extremely happy years. In 1952 I knew only that I wanted a job where I could make an impact, and that meant seeking out a relatively 'small pool'. Although I worked for the whole of local government, and had a significant period in the Civil Service, my 'pool' remained small. That is because I stuck to the core of my expertise in consumer affairs. I was at the fulcrum point of change for thirty-five years and oversaw or negotiated significant changes in management, consumer law and public relations. I ought to record some of the history and background to inform professional colleagues. But there are so many events, and so many stories, I am still trying to summon the energy to begin.

Ron Gainsford, Lynne Skelton, Suresh Gopenathan, my staff and colleagues, gave me a marvellous retirement send-off at the Royal Academy of Fine Arts. Fire engines arrived. Silver balloons with my face were released down the Strand and across Trafalgar Square. People said kind things and there seemed to be a large gathering of ministers, civil servants, chairmen, councillors, officials, chief officers, students and staff, past and present. I was proud to have my family there in strength and to be able to hold my first lovely grandchild, nine-months-old James Paterson - an emotional delight reminiscent of the parade of Josephine (his mother) at the age of six months around a Kano supermarket in June 1964.

My official retirement opened new opportunities. My friend and the new Minister of Trade, Nigel Griffiths MP, was responsible when I was appointed to the board of the National Consumer Council. The Minister of Health appointed me to the Wine Standards Board. I thoroughly enjoyed both appointments and think I was able to make some telling contributions. I also felt well honoured to have been made Vice-President of the Trading Standards Institute (TSi), a body so important and central to the whole of my professional life.

In May 2003 I was diagnosed with an aggressive form of prostate cancer. In December 2004 Freda was diagnosed with Alzheimer's. We both remain relaxed, happy and phlegmatic and intend to make full use of our twilight years. Radiotherapy and hormone drugs seem to have currently blitzed the cancer. Freda has been prescribed the controversial Aricept drug by the Croydon Memory Clinic and it seems to be proving an effective retardant. She recently gave a moving address on the effects of Alzheimer's to an international medical conference at Fairfield Halls, Croydon.

I have become a member of the Board of Dignity in Dying, and have always believed in freedom of choice for end-of-life decisions. We campaign for strict controls to ensure that the decision to end life is legally restricted to competent persons with terminal illnesses suffering unbearable pain. It is a concept quite different from euthanasia which means others make terminal decisions on your behalf.

I am also a Trustee of Golden Leaves – for pre-paid funerals – and the Orator of the TSi College of Fellows, the charitable wing of the trading standards profession. I am happy they are jobs 'appropriate to my situation' and a far cry from the whirl of business trips abroad, broadcasting and professional rugby. Opera, golf and bridge with close friends Gordon Lees and Gerry Dodd (the 'Humble-Tumble League') remain the recreations I most enjoy, as well as many and more holidays: great holidays with Ann and Eric Bolton or our daughters and seven lovely grandchildren James, Ben, Alice, Sam, Thomas, Emily and Elliot. They are quite wonderful.

I have rejoined the British Humanist Association. I was a member many years ago, stimulated by the author Aldous Huxley. Debates with Freda's Aunty Nene about her Catholicism merely served to strengthen my convictions. The BHA philosophies seem so much more rational, acceptable and sensible than the mystical, unbelievable beliefs of the faith communities.

And now I have much more time to listen and play... and write these notes... than I had when my daughters were in their adolescence.

FINALLY FREDA

Freda Holden was born 20 May 1937 and lived with mother, father, elder sister Shirley and younger brother Robin at 24 Meadow Lane, Garden Suburb, Oldham. She attended Oldham Hulme Grammar School. She first experimented with a career in shorthand and typing and then worked at the chemist Timothy, White and Taylor before qualifying as a hairdresser in Manchester. This was not her vocation and with her mother's encouragement she qualified as a teacher at the Charlotte Mason College in Ambleside.

I fell under her spell in 1958 whilst she was doing teaching practice at Werneth School in Oldham. I determined there and then that she was the girl I would marry. It was another three years before we spoke (see 'Courtship' chapter) but my enthusiasm was undiminished. She says I 'pursued her relentlessly' and she is probably right, as I never had the slightest doubt that we would raise a family and spend the rest of our lives together. That view remains unchallenged.

Freda is a very special person. Her father told me she would 'make a perky wife'. She is far more than that. She is outspoken, has a bubbling personality, is confrontational, adventurous and confident with high ethical and moral standards. I admired all these traits, many of which – in particular her outspokenness - complemented weaknesses of my own: I mostly avoid confrontation and seek quiet consensus. I doubt if I would have accepted my career-changing job in Africa without Freda's enthusiastic encouragement.

In the early stages of my career she sharpened my draughtsmanship, improved my official reports and, as an audience of one, prepared me for interviews and speeches. I came to rely on her judgement, absolutely.

Freda had become an insulin dependent diabetic at the age of eleven years. It was an embarrassing issue at the time. She squirmed when having to refuse sweets and cakes from friends' mothers and, later, her 'tipple' with sophisticated boyfriends was a vile-tasting neat gin. Fruit drinks and mixers had added sugar. She suffered agonies trying to keep her diabetes a secret. Sixty years later both Freda and I remember that lesson. Friends and family were told immediately about our Alzheimer's and cancer and the immediate relief from stress, and related agonies, has been a therapeutic bonus.

Our married life has not been without hiccups along the way but I have never, at any point, ceased to respect and admire Freda... whatever the provocation! There are no regrets. She is a wonderful mother, a wonderful partner. I love her still.

PHOTOGRAPHS

Top
Thomas and Tamar Rhodes (maternal grandparents of the author) with children Alice (the author's mother) and Fred, 1925.

Bottom left
Joseph and Hannah Humble (paternal grandparents of the author) with babies Jenny and Fred, 1907.

Bottom right
Joseph 'Joe' Humble, the author's father, 1926.

Top
Jimmy Humble aged 9, his sister Margaret aged 2, and his mother Alice Humble, 1945.

Centre left
Jimmy and Margaret Humble. Prize photo. Blackpool, 1949.

Centre right
Alice and Joe, Jimmy's happy parents, 1990.

Bottom, from left to right
Josephine aged 10, Rebecca aged 9 and Sarah aged 8, daughters of Jimmy Humble.

Top left
Wedding of Joseph Humble and Alice Rhodes, Jimmy's parents, August 1935.

Top right
Wedding of James Humble (the author) and Freda Holden, April 1962.

Bottom left
Freda Holden, 1961.

Bottom right
Jimmy Humble, Leigh v Wigan, 1960.

Top left
Margaret, sister of the author, with Jamie the dog.

Top right
James K Humble OBE with Rebecca, Freda and Sarah, Buckingham Palace, 1993.

Bottom
Grandad Jimmy Humble's 70th birthday, Norfolk, 8 May 2006. As well as Freda and Jimmy (central), the family group includes (left to right) sons-in-law Stanley Munson, David Cordle and Martin Paterson; daughters Sarah, Josephine (standing) and Rebecca (seated); and grandchildren James Paterson, Ben Paterson, Alice Munson, Sam Paterson, Thomas Munson and Emily Cordle. Note: Elliot Cordle not yet born.

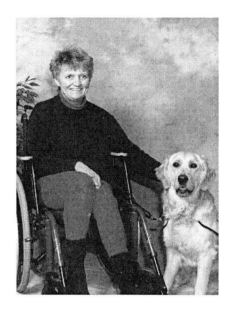

APPENDIX A: MEMORIES OF MY MOTHER

Letter from Alice Rhodes to Rebecca (1989)

I was born 22nd October 1908 and am just 80 years of age. Nancy (Holden) is busy with family trees and suggested I write something to my grandchild Rebecca about my life and family, most now dead and gone.

Dear Becca... ...
Hannah and George Sykes, my grandparents, had five living children. The eldest, a girl called Tamar, was my mother. Hannah in her prime weighed 20 stone and when she was old and shrivelled I used to sit on her knee and count her many many chins. George, my grandfather, was always called 'Judd' and had a pet bulldog. Soon after my brother Fred was born the bulldog carried him off by his night-dress and put him on the mat. 'Judd' also bred Pomeranian dogs and canaries and I remember the bulldog and several canaries were stuffed and displayed on the sideboard in a glass case. Grandfather sometimes smoked a clay pipe and was a renowned Lancashire clog dancer. His brother demonstrated clog dancing in America.

They lived in Trafalgar Street, Oldham near to my parents Tamar and Tom Rhodes, Fred and I who at first lived in Mitchell Street. There were no old age pensions and everyone dreaded becoming destitute and having to end their days in the 'Workhouse'. Many men and women dressed in rags; they sang in the street and begged for money. I loved to be able to give them pennies. Sometimes a man called 'Pea Harry' called at the house with steaming hot black peas. It cost one penny for a lovely supper. Italians begged with barrel organs and a pet monkey dressed in a red coat held out a tin for pennies. When I was very young I remember a man begging with a dancing, or shuffling, brown bear on the end of a chain.

Mother used to tell me stories about the Boer War, about Queen Victoria, and her own hard life in the card room at the Mill. She started full-time work when she was only 10 years old.

When Tom Rhodes, my father, was a young man he came near to death but had one of the very first successful appendicitis operations in 1914. He was cut from neck to naval and always had a poor appetite and bowel trouble. He had to wear a special belt and steel plate to support his innards. When the 1914 World War broke out he was distressed to be classed C3 not A1. He was advised to find work out of doors. Electric trams were just starting to run through the main streets of Oldham and he became a tram driver. They ran on lines and had an overhead trolley connected to a 'live' wire. The front and back of the trams were open and passengers exposed to all weathers. As a boy he hated going to school and often ran away. However he loved reading, particularly Shakespeare, singing in a good, but light, tenor voice and taking us long walks on the moors above Oldham. From there we could see hundreds of smoking factory chimneys.

Father was a teetotaller and virtual non-smoker. Therefore we never really mixed with father's brothers or sisters because most of them liked 'boozing'. Father had a fresh complexion and a ginger moustache. He always used to rub mentholated spirits into his face to keep it smooth and for the 'fresh air' treatment. He spent ages preening if we went on an outing and there was often a row if mother had ironed a crease into his stiffly starched collar. He was a very strong and active supporter of the Labour movement and the trade unions. We loved to sing 'The Red Flag'. His heroes were politicians Ramsay MacDonald and JR Clynes. [Editor's note: John Robert Clynes (1869 – 1949), leader of the Labour Party, was born in Oldham and worked in a cotton mill. He and Tom Rhodes were contemporaries and are very likely to have been associates.]

I will next try to describe our next house at 64 Hanson Street, a typical workman's four-roomed terraced house where I lived until I was married in 1935. There was a sitting room, a living kitchen, a stone cellar and two bedrooms (no bathroom). Outside, a small stone backyard, water closet and coal bunker. The paintwork and doors were all dull brown. Even clothes and materials were all dark drab colours, to save washing. Shoes and stockings were black. In the living kitchen the whole of one wall was built up with a black iron fireplace, oven and boiler with some small brass and steel adornments. The whole monstrosity had to be blackleaded and polished and polished every week.

In the corner was a boiler with another fireplace underneath. This is where any white clothes were boiled and sterilised. Other dirty clothes were placed in a wooden tub and 'possed' to loosen the dirt with a Posser (a large wooden stick), rubbed on a Rubbing Board and scrubbed on the Slop Stone under cold water (a large sandstone sink with low sides). The clothes were squeezed through a huge Mangling Machine and hung to dry… all over the house if it was raining. My biggest hatred was steaming wet clothes taking away the cosy warmth of the kitchen. There were no washing machines and even the lighting was by a fragile gas mantle.

All the cooking including potato pies, roasts, puddings, bread and oven-bottom muffins were done in the oven next to the fire. My memory is that food has never tasted so delicious. In the morning we were woken by the 'Knockers Up'. A man had a long pole with wire looped at the top. He tapped on the bedroom windows to waken the cotton mill workers. The lassies wore clogs and shawls and the lads had caps and mufflers. The fashion was to carry a basin of lunch tied into a red spotted handkerchief.

I best loved Oldham Wakes, our annual general holiday. There were roundabouts, huge steam boats, throwing games and exhibitions of freaks: the Fat Lady, two-headed animals and Siamese twins. I paid to see the 'Tiny Fairy' and was very disappointed to see just a small, very old lady dressed in fairy clothes. We played around lampposts in the streets. Girls played hop flag, whip and top and skipping rope. The boys played marbles, with kites, and balls and peggy, a pointed top flipped off a brick and hit as far as possible. Many children had a foot cycle and in winter there was always snow sledges and skating on the frozen Park Lake. There were no cars and we played very safely in the streets. Horses clip-clopped everywhere, carthorses hauling huge trucks with bags of coal and horses and traps delivering milk from a churn. We went to the door with either a pint or quart jug for whatever we wanted.

In the First World War, 1914-1918, I learned to knit khaki scarves, mittens, socks and balaclavas for the soldiers in the trenches. I was under 10 years old and have never stopped enjoying knitting. During the War our family spent a week's holiday at New Brighton (near Liverpool). It was very exciting because we were near a fort with cannons and searchlights moving over the sands. My brother and I caused trouble because we tore up small pieces of paper to throw and reflect in the searchlight beam. The soldiers shouted and yelled and we were told to keep away. I thought I was going to be shot or bayoneted as a spy. We all did drawings of the hated German Kaiser with his turned-up pointed moustache, a point on his head and his little son Willie by his side.

Everywhere there were posters with Lord Kitchener's eyes, pointing and saying "We Want You". Young men who didn't volunteer for the army were secretly given a 'white feather'. I thought this was very cruel because it meant they were cowards.

My Uncle Walter served in the Tank Corps and an Uncle Richard was killed on the day the Armistice was declared. My mother's most handsome brother Samuel was a sergeant in the Canadian Army. He convalesced in England after being seriously wounded in the jaw and was fitted with an intricate gold and metal contraption inside his mouth with a wheel at the top and another at the bottom. This allowed his jaw to be moved by hand so that he could chew and eat.

Mother's youngest sister Sarah Alice (Sh'ralice) and her husband Gerard Booth were my godparents. They went to live at Weymouth as Uncle Gerard worked at Portland Bill making torpedoes. I went to live with them for 12 months because Aunty was lonely and didn't know anyone. I attended school in Weymouth. It was 1917; I was 9 years old. The train journey to the South took forever and we went via the Severn Tunnel; it was very black, no lights and I was very frightened when sparks flew past the window. There were no corridors and no toilets on the train.

In Weymouth we once took a rowing boat into the bay. Aunty rowed but the sea became rough and we were swept away from the shore. Uncle dared not move to take the oars in case he overturned the boat. Aunty was weak and sick; I was afraid. But we lived to tell the tale.

In Oldham we always had to queue in the shops when food arrived. My special job was always the potatoes. I particularly hated the bread queue because the bread was such a dirty grey colour.

After the War two cousins were my most special friends. Aunty Rachel and Uncle Walter had a confectioner's shop in Lees Road and had one daughter Evelyn. Later they had a boarding house in Blackpool in Waverley Avenue. I went for very happy holidays and if they had no visitors I slept in the best bedroom, the Five-shilling Room. Otherwise it was the attic, the Halfpenny Room. Wonderful times. We were like sisters and still keep in touch. Father's brother Sam Rhodes had three children, and Velma, the eldest, was just a few months older. We were both in the same class at Clarksfield

School. We looked alike but she was very confident and taught me 'the facts of life'. She had elocution lessons and spoke well and was given the part of Oberon in the school play, A Midsummer Night's Dream. She successfully begged the teachers to allow me to play Titania. Her father Sam worked at Asa Lees Iron Works and made two wonderful iron crowns.

Velma and I were in the scholarship class. We had very good teachers with a reputation of gaining the best scholarships in the town. However my teachers were disgusted because my mother refused to allow me even to sit the scholarship examination. They summonsed my mother to school but she refused to budge. She acknowledged that Fred, my brother, had got a scholarship but insisted 'one's enough in any family'. In fact my mother initially objected to Fred taking a scholarship even though he was 'top' of the school. However the Headmaster got involved and got her to change her mind. I remember it being very upsetting. Every other child in my class secured a scholarship.

In fact I had not been particularly thrilled with school and quite happily went to Waterloo Higher Standard Centre for Domestic Education. I just loved needlework, dressmaking, cookery and domestic science. When I left I was presented with a prize, a large volume of Mrs Beeton's cookery book for gaining highest marks in the Lancashire and Cheshire Examinations.

I think my lifelong love of needlework and crocheting was derived from my much-loved Aunt Alice. She worked with great speed and crocheted round tablecloths, pillowslips, tam-O-shanties and 'hug me' tights and even on fine white cotton underwear. The tablecloths were beautifully patterned with cups, saucers, sugar tongs, spoons and even cream jugs. She stitched around the bottom of my petticoats and bloomers. On Whit Friday all the Sunday School children processioned around the streets in their new clothes. We then went to show off to neighbours, relatives and friends and hoped to collect gifts of money. My skirts were constantly being turned up so that people could admire the wonderful crochet work on my underwear.

When anyone died all the neighbours and relatives visited the house to view the body. The corpse was dressed in a beautiful white satin sheet and laid out on a table or in a coffin. I went with my mother to pay last respects to a young girlfriend who had drowned in a nearby reservoir. I was deeply shocked she was so changed with her face swollen and discoloured. If not invited, we children would gather around the door to watch the mourners dressed in black. A most magnificent pair of black horses drew each funeral coach.

I started work in 1924 just before my 15th birthday and was keen to 'serve my time' in a sewing workshop. Initially my wage was 6/6d [Editor's note: six shillings and six pence equal to 32½p] a week rising slightly each year until I had finished my apprenticeship. This took five years and then I became a fully-fledged tailoress. I specialised in making men's suits. A lot of patience was required doing hand sewing, basting, filling and hand buttonholes. I was very happy working at the Oldham Equitable Coop with 20 or more girls, a couple of youths, two tailors and our one-legged foreman. The two tailors sat cross-legged on top of the tables and their job was just to hand sew the most expensive lounge jackets. Our one machine worker was a particularly exuberant midget, called Clarice.

Some bits of my young life were difficult, particularly relationships with my parents. If we went out as a family, brother Fred and I had to hold hands and walk in front. We could only speak when we were spoken to and must not touch dirty walls or stub our shoes. We had to do what we were told immediately, must never 'answer back' and respect all our elders.

As a child I only ever hung a stocking, not a pillowcase, on Christmas Eve. I was thrilled to receive just a penny, an orange and a book or perhaps a small bottle of perfume. When I was working I saved for a summer holiday but also wanted a tennis racquet to play with my friends. I got the racquet but my holiday was cancelled.

Mother died the year Josephine was born, 1964, when she was 84 years. Looking back I do not think I ever defied her, argued with her or sought to displease her. I always strove to make her happy in any way I could. I guess I must be a very submissive sort of person but think I have always been happy and grateful for whatever treats came my way.

APPENDIX B: LETTERS FROM NIGERIA

Edited by Nancy Holden (mother-in-law of James Humble) (1963)

Jimmy to Humbles (Nigeria 16.2.1963)
Five more days and we will have finished yet another safari around the country. Our car and landrover are loaded to the eyes because we have stayed with friends, in rest houses, bush huts, tents and even two nights in a de-luxe hotel. We carry everything from candles and cookware to evening dresses and bow tie plus all the metrological testing equipment. Garaba (our steward) disappeared to Zaria a few days before we left, to organise the funeral of his brother-in-law. Very irritating that he didn't return in time for the trip but we can manage, and at least didn't have to fit in his entire luggage.

The first day out of Kano we drove 350 long hot miles to Gombe. It was the first day after the harmattan and it was like living in a steam oven. Thick clouds of dust rose from the laterite road and in the first hour clothes, hair and everything inside the car was thick with orange dust... Work is easier now as I can trust the student Inspectors to inspect on their own in the cotton markets. We saw our first pagans in large numbers on this trip. Heads completely shaven, leaves fore and aft twitching in the breeze, and pendulous breasts which the women tuck under an arm when feeding children on their backs. Saw three ostriches and stopped close to photograph. Later found they could be quite dangerous.

In Gombe I had to interview the Chief Constable who had been testing 200lb spring balances with a single 28lb weight. He was putting some traders in jail if the scale wasn't correct to 8oz. The Federal laws allow 2lb errors and the police have no powers. The traders told me that the Chief Constable took 'dash' (bribes) and if a market trader didn't pay him £3-£5 he found some pretext for prison. I am discovering bribery is everywhere. An ordinary constable who wants to be a gate-man at a market must pay his inspector £25-£40 for the posting. A constable's wages are £2 per week so I guess he also takes bribes. Several people told me about the Chief Constable. Three years ago, then an inspector, he arrested a thief for stealing £700. He split the money £500 for himself and £200 for the robber before allowing the robber to escape. The news leaked and he was convicted and sent to prison for two years. Six months ago he was released and now he is Chief Constable. No one here seems surprised.

From Gombe we went to Bauchi and planned the weekend in a tented camp to meet jungle cats on their own terms. Two punctures and only one spare wheel was a bad start but we left camp at first dawn armed with cameras and enthusiasm. Three hours later we returned dispirited having seen only one grey shape which might, or might not, have been a pig. About 150 ft below our camp was a beautiful crystal-clear, pale blue spring, the size of a large swimming pool, called Wikki Warm Water Spring. At dusk we hung two tilley lamps on overhanging trees and bathed in the warm water for hours. We slept under thick and heavy mosquito nets and could pick out the howls of hyenas, barks of baboons and the roars of the cats.

The following day we left at 5am but saw only two king porcupine and a lynx. But Day 3 we saw animals aplenty: monkeys, wild pig, many baboons, deer, dyka and bush cow. We sat on top of the landrover when a large herd of bush cow charged in front of us. We hammered for the driver to go faster and only adrenaline stopped us falling off as he chased the thundering beasts. My friend David Evans was bitten by tsetse flies and was covered from head to toe in huge red bites. Freda and I were bitten but there were no marks. Funny.

Our next port of call was Yom on the high plateau in the centre of Nigeria. It was lush and green and peopled by many naked (and beautiful) people. Many of the women had huge lips which had been stretched by heavy metal studs. Later discovered they were the 'platypus' women and the disfigurement was done to make them too ugly to be caught by slave traders. Within the tribe the lips are now considered things of beauty. We stayed the night in their straw-covered huts with lots of cockroaches and bats.

Freda acquired a dog from one of my students. He's called Whisky. We are teaching him to bark. From Yom we travelled to Jos and the famous five-star Hill Station Hotel at £100 per night. Big problem: "No Dogs Allowed". When I was out the Manager found "Modom" was hiding Whisky dog under our bed and we were banished to distant chalets normally used by travellers with children. Nevertheless it was a wonderful experience and fantastic menu.

From Jos we plunged off the Plateau to Wamba: hot, sticky and humid, with our bodies permanently soaked in perspiration. From Wamba to Abuja and the famous potters and then our landrover broke down (again) at Keffi on the banks of the Niger. We have a broken half-shaft (the driver put it into reverse whilst travelling forward) and have no idea how we can make the last 400 miles to Kano. That's why I'm writing this letter. On our trip we have so far covered 4,200 miles, had four breakdowns, three slashed tyres and now this half-shaft... and we have also seized more than 100 spring balances with the coils fraudulently altered and 80 platform scales with secretly added lead weights and... have earned enough money to pay all our year's salaries from official verification fees.

Jimmy to Holdens (Kano 24.02.63)
We are excited awaiting a visit from Bill, Shirley and baby Nichola. [Editor's note: The Stonebridges: brother-in-law and sister to Freda.] They are moving from Mokwa to live permanently in Kano next month. Today is Garaba's day off and Freda is preparing pork chops and onions in the quite horrid kitchen. Europeans usually avoid Nigerian pork because of lurid tales of tapeworm. However a Danish friend has started a pig farm in Kano so we will give him some business.

Our friends in Kano see us as very experienced travellers 'cos we have crossed and criss-crossed the country looking for every kind of commercial enterprise: groundnut markets, cotton gins, rubber plantations, coffee, tobacco, gold and spices. In six months Freda and I have already toured more than 20,000 miles on laterite roads, stone roads, drift-sand roads and dried-up riverbeds. Worst are the car-destroying corrugated roads which shake bones and metal to destruction. We are very pleased we chose the well-sprung Peugeot 404 car which also has a strong frame. Pity no British manufacturer is yet able to produce a car fit for the roads in these newly developing African countries.

We went to the English Anglican Church this morning and sat in the congregation of nine. Unfortunately the vicar didn't appear and people sidled out one by one. We were the 7th and 8th to leave. However the African Anglican churches are packed to the doors with huge overflows singing and dancing at every window. I went instead to train for the rugby season with our new dog Whisky trotting behind. The locals hooted with laughter to see so much energy being uselessly wasted, on a Sunday, in such a hot, sticky climate.

Yesterday we went to the Sallah of Katsina (town north of Kano) on the edge of the Sahara. I wore my best white suit. The Sallah is the celebration to end the fasting of Muslims and each tribal chief in his region salutes the Emir with his own 'army' of colourfully dressed horsemen. Each group of horsemen, twenty or thirty abreast, charge at the Emir on his tented throne and then rear up the horses just a few feet away. We were sitting right behind the Emir. There is enormous noise and screams and time and time again we got covered with gut-wrenching dust...

Jimmy to Humbles (Kano 16.3.63)
My students and labourers seem to exist on almost nothing, usually two identical meals a day of garri soup (garri is a root crop). If they feel hungry they just chew a cola nut about the size of a large walnut. We eventually got back

from tour and I borrowed money to pay for £93 repairs to the landrover and £27 for my car. The Nescafe we brought from England has just finished, but the one tin lasted almost six months. We can't afford a replacement; they are 47/6d each. [Editor's note: forty-seven shillings and six pence, equal to £2.37½.] We are due a long tour in the West of Nigeria in two weeks' time but I have had a message from Lagos: "No more Touring". It seems the Federal Government has no money until the new financial year April/May. Hope they might then be able to repay my £300 travel costs.

Remember I told you about the forged bags of Pillsbury Flour. We have been finding them in all kinds of markets and local shops and one trader was foolish enough to tell me where the forged bags are made. The trail leads to an address in Jos. I can't travel, but I'm sending two students, three policemen and the trader 500 miles to bring me back a prisoner... a forger. They did catch the forger and I prosecuted him 12 months later in an Alkali Court based on native law and custom. We sat on a marble floor; every word spoken was laboriously written by three scribes; it was tediously slow and people came in and out of Court to sell nuts, soft drinks and newspapers. The forger got five years in prison. [Note: In 2007 I discovered this had been one of the radical Sharia Courts, now much in the news.]

Freda is getting inspired to teach again. The sessions on tour with local children have whetted her appetite. She has phoned all the schools in Kano. The Heads want her... but have first got to get government clearance that no Nigerian girl is available to do her job.

With work limited, we have time to play tennis at the Kano Club or badminton in our laterite garden. The garden boy and I have built quite a good court. Dad would be proud. One of my students Abdul Balogun has helped and he is quite a good player. This takes the competitive pressure off Freda. The Kano Club is quite posh with mostly European members. The Nigerians think it's crazy to pay such expensive imported prices for their drinks. I share their opinion.

My beard and Freda's hair are getting longer and longer. Only our good manners and proud bearing (joke) prevent us being mistaken for beatniks! We have started to play bridge and I am teaching five other couples. The problem is that they all want to invite us out for dinner (and lessons) and it is getting quite exhausting.

Jimmy to Humbles and Holdens (Kano 1.3.63)
The Emir of Kano has resigned. I don't suppose it seems important in England but in Kano it's a sensation. It's like the abdication of the Queen. It seems he has been caught dipping into the native authority money to the tune of several hundred thousand pounds. Papers show he has a fleet of sixty cars and his annual car claim is equivalent to every car driving at 60mph for 365 days, 24 hours a day. Just read Geoffrey Bing's book about government in Ghana. He argues corruption is fine as it substitutes for proper social services. Everybody knows the leaders and managers cheat and take bribes but that money is then trickled down to villages and families etc. I'm not convinced. [Editor's note: The publication Jimmy read in 1963 will have been a precursor to Geoffrey Bing's memoir 'Reap the Whirlwind:

an Account of Kwame Nkrumah's Ghana from 1950 to 1966'
(MacGibbon & Kee, 1968).]

Freda has started work at the Kano Convent School and
loves it. The girls are quiet, well behaved and eager to learn.
It seems to have a very soothing environment and her salary
is a whopping £760 p.a. We have been able to buy a
Mobylette (a scooter-cum-autocycle) which is great to whizz
in and around Kano and for Freda to get to and from school.

Sad news in that Garaba has been accepted for the army.
He is hard-working and efficient, always happy and good to
be with. We shall miss him. He has just told me he was never
in Zaria to organise his brother-in-law's funeral. He missed
our Safari in February because he was doing basic army
training and the entrance tests! I can't be cross. Seems he
had to buy the answers from the Sabon Gari market.
Everything can be bought in the market from human skulls
to GCE questions. He also had to bribe the clerk who gave
him his application forms, the Intelligence Test Examiner,
the Sergeant Major who judged his physical fitness and the
male nurse who tested his urine. Sad but we wish him well.
It must be better than being a servant… if he survives. He
is producing a short list of house stewards to take over his
position.

VERY LAST WORD

I had approving reports in the Civil Service although one complained I was "(too) enthusiastic and professional". This implied I might succumb to prejudice or bias. Local government saw these as virtues to be applauded and that is where I felt more comfortable.

I have had a life with no extraordinary highs or devastating lows. But I have had happiness, and good fortune, and tried to take advantage of every opportunity. I know I have worked hard, worked conscientiously and tackled tasks, great and small, to the very best of my abilities.

I am an optimist. In making decisions I anticipate the most favourable outcome. This is not necessarily wise, but I long ago discovered it was a recipe for halving disappointment. Friends and colleagues with a contrary view often seemed to suffer twice: first in the anticipation of disappointment and then again if things went wrong.

I have always tried to respect and understand the views of my peers, friends and opponents, even when those views ran counter to my own. This may often have led to 'fence-sitting' but it was an asset in a career devoted to achieving change, compromise, consensus and conciliation.

If I had a second chance, I would do the same.

Who can say more?

James K Humble

FAMILY TREES

FAMILY TREE
Humble 1616-1936

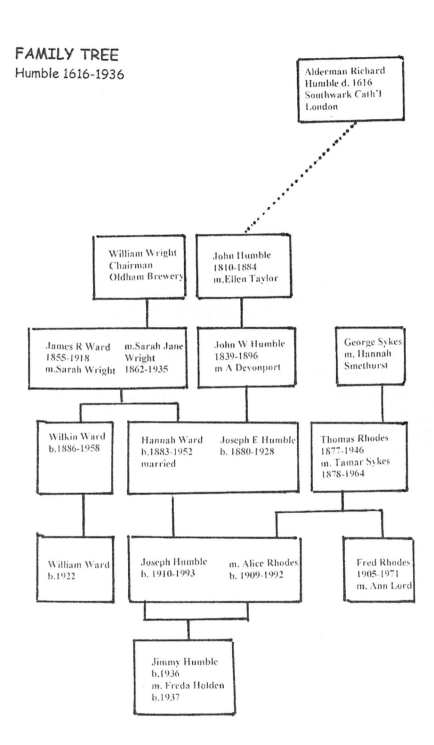

Alderman Richard Humble d. 1616 Southwark Cath'l London

William Wright Chairman Oldham Brewery

John Humble 1810-1884 m.Ellen Taylor

James R Ward 1855-1918 m.Sarah Wright

m.Sarah Jane Wright 1862-1935

John W Humble 1839-1896 m A Devonport

George Sykes m. Hannah Smethurst

Wilkin Ward b.1886-1958

Hannah Ward b.1883-1952 married

Joseph E Humble b. 1880-1928

Thomas Rhodes 1877-1946 m. Tamar Sykes 1878-1964

William Ward b.1922

Joseph Humble b. 1910-1993

m. Alice Rhodes b. 1909-1992

Fred Rhodes 1905-1971 m. Ann Lord

Jimmy Humble b.1936 m. Freda Holden b.1937

FAMILY TREE
Humble 1903-2008

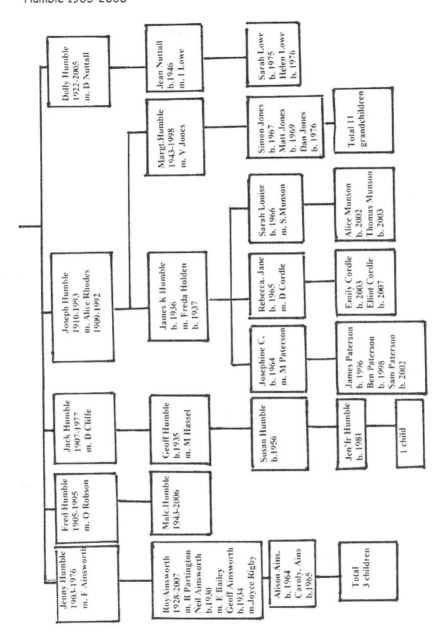